the

Maju

MINDSET

May you always have
the courage to follow
your heart

the

Maju

MINDSET

GOODBYE BULLSHIT. HELLO HAPPY!

A MODERN GUIDE FOR GETTING OUT OF
YOUR OWN DAMN WAY

KRISTI LEE SCHATZ, MACP

Maju Global, LLC
Attn: Kristi Lee Schatz
1662 Stockton Street, Suite 206
Jacksonville, FL 32204
www.MajuLife.com

ISBN-13: 978-1535289245

Cover design by Jeffery Harrington of Harrington Design Company
Edited by Caren Burmeister

Printed in the United States of America.

This book is dedicated to the next generation.
May those who walk before you have the courage to face their fears and truly model how to be a loving human being. This is all for you.

CONTENTS

ACKNOWLEDGMENTS

To my unconditionally loving parents, Ed and Dale Schatz, who support me every time I trust my intuition and take a leap of faith. Thank you for always encouraging me to be my best and brightest self in this world. You are my sunshine and I wish all parents could embody the gift of acceptance you have given me. Thank you.

To Sue Kornhauser, Leigh-Ann Sullivan, Jordan Myska-Allen, Sara Ness, Amy Silverman, Celeste Blackman, Dr. Keith Holden, Jeffery Harrington, Caren Burmeister, and Natasha Dern: this book wouldn't be the same without all of your contributions. Thank you!

To my incredible support system of friends, family, teachers, and colleagues around the world: thank you for feeding my soul and opening my heart. I love you all.

To my inner child: thanks for being a badass!

When the children roam free once more,

the world will be free to live again.

-Kristi Lee Schatz

DO IT FOR THE CHILDREN
(DO NOT SKIP THIS FOLKS)

T his is a call to action. It's time to do something different; not just for yourself, but for the wellbeing of the next generation. Our presence is energy and the young absorbent minds are taking it all in, watching and mirroring the way we move through life. Our habitual autopilot reactions, judgments, limiting beliefs, and stress - they see and feel it all. What are they absorbing from you, their schools, their peers, and the media? Are they seeing compassion, acceptance, patience, and self-love in action? Or are they witnessing resentment, ridicule, and a life out of balance? What did you witness growing up and how did it impact you?

Our lives have become chaotic and our minds are overwhelmed. We've become creatures of habit, reacting to the environment with little to no awareness of the impact we are having on the world around us. While we are not responsible for managing other people's emotions, we are responsible for managing our own.

The quality of your presence influences the depth of your relationships and life experiences. The way you show up, the grace in which you handle tough situations, your boundaries, and the permission you give yourself to be authentic and vulnerable are all mirrors for others to reflect upon. When you embody your true self, you demonstrate to the world what is possible.

Adjusting your lens of reality to include the possibility that your potential might actually be limitless is critical to your personal wellbeing. It's also an imperative awareness that we must seed in the consciousness of the next generation. Co-creating a world that operates from a space of lack and limitation, projection and judgment, and inauthentic connection not only restricts our ability to tap our creative potential, but models to the precious young minds how to think and react to the world around them. Let's ensure the next generation doesn't have the same experience as us. We have the tools, research, and countless testimonials of radical transformation that proves the power of stepping out of our comfort zone and doing something different. So what if no one ever taught us these essential life skills when we growing up. They didn't know, but we do. When you take steps to evolve yourself on purpose you produce a ripple in the fabric of our social consciousness. Your presence is your power and the catalyst to transforming future generations.

Truth be told, this book calls bullshit on several personal and societal norms that are likely part of your daily life. These ideas may challenge you, inspire you, or completely piss you off. All of those responses are perfect because I trust your process is exactly the experience you need to have. I am shining a light on my deep truths because they are the perspectives that saved my life.

I use to suffer from severe depression and debilitating anxiety. Most people didn't know I was in pain because I hid it so well. I had to be perfect. I had to fit in. I couldn't possibly let others know how overactive my mind was so I silently suffered alone. I feared judgment and confrontation and tried to live up to everyone's expectations. I never felt good enough and I almost lost my life from a lack of self-love. Fortunately, everything changed when I began to integrate the concepts I share in this book. I am now a vibrant and passionate woman with a sense of purpose living each day to the fullest. I feel like a completely different person living an extraordinary life. If I can change as much as I have, anyone can.

This book is nothing shy of a personal reveal. The insights shared are my truths. Take what resonates, chew on what challenges you, and discard what doesn't feel right. Publishing a book this real, raw, and vividly exposing is by far the most vulnerable thing I have experienced to date. The ups, the downs, and humiliating moments of growth culminate to make me who I am today. I am a passionate and outspoken advocate for personal and societal evolution because I have witnessed firsthand the detrimental effects of being raised by a society on autopilot. I refuse to stand by and watch another generation be raised in a climate that perpetuates projection, disconnection, and a fear of authentic self-expression.

The perspectives I share in this book are seeds of possibility for a new way of relating to the world. I place the paint brush of creation smack dab in your hands. If you're feeling unfulfilled by the way your life is currently going and you're truly ready to thrive, then this is your time to shine. When you give yourself permission to fully show up and dance with life, others will follow suit. This book is not only meant to get you thinking about how your way of being impacts the quality of your life, but how it affects the system as a whole.

No one is perfect and that isn't the intention. This is about actively engaging in the unfolding process of your life from exactly where you stand now. You are capable of creating an extraordinary life beyond what your mind tells you is possible. But you must first make the choice to get out of your own damn way.

As you read this book, you will notice my conversational tone is a mix of being loving yet tough, with a few sprinkles of profanity and a dash of playfulness. By nature, I want to coddle you and let you know I see you, that you're not alone, and we're all in this together. But, at the same time, I want to smack you across the face with a feather and tell you to wake up. Why? Because I wish someone had done it for me sooner. I wish I would have had more unconditionally loving role models who had walked the trench of vulnerability and had seen the magnificence on the other side. I wish they would have shown me the possibility that I am limitless and the only thing holding me back were the constructs of my own mind. I wish they would have consciously leaned into my edge of discomfort because I was too stuck in my habitual way of being to do it myself.

I didn't need teachers telling me how to be or what to think. I needed them to embody the virtues of authenticity, vulnerability, personal responsibly, and trust. I needed to see them walk their talk and model the possibilities of living a truly extraordinary life and hold space for me to show up in my own unique way. Would I have believed them if they told me that it was safe to step outside of my comfort zone and show my true self to the world? Maybe. Maybe not. But that's not the point. If we don't have embodied, authentic role models dancing through society to begin with, we will all continue to fumble without awareness of how we are collectively contributing to the chaos. Don't get me wrong, my family of origin is probably the coolest group of people on this planet. We play together, fumble together, and grow together. This is less about my family system, and more about the health of society as a whole. No matter what you've learned, you have the power to recreate your story.

We were all dealt a different set of cards. Some pick up a solid foundation of emotional intelligence, others are dealt an ego-centric and ethno-centric worldview and a blind spot for their own privilege. Some are born into extreme poverty and an obvious disadvantage right out of the gate. Comparing yourself to others, whether you place them above or below yourself, perpetuates disconnection and does absolutely nothing for anyone's wellbeing.

The Maju Mindset is a way of relating to life. It's about being present where you are at this very moment without judgment. It's about learning to listen and trust the inner whisper asking you to step forward in whatever way is right for you. It's about dissolving the audio tape of society's voice and choosing to cultivate the presence you wish to see flourish in the world. This isn't about becoming the next shining star in your job, community, or industry. Of course you can do that and it will be epic. This is about you being embodied in your day to day life as a warrior for change. It's about the kids on the playground who smile when you walk by because they recognize you as a light in the darkness. This journey is about walking your talk and owning your shit, because that's when everything else will fall into place.

Maju, you ask? The term comes from the Malay language and means to advance, progress or move forward. The word lends itself beautifully to the notion that developing yourself as an individual will evolve the system as a whole. As you move forward, so does the world.

A few statements of forewarning:

1. I swear like a sailor in this book (hence the subtitle). Sometimes there are only certain words that convey the energy of what I'm actually feeling. I'm totally innocent at my core, but really enjoy the freedom of letting it all out authentically. Plus, we can all relate to dealing with bullshit.

2. This book may shake your foundation and possibly even shatter your worldview in the best way possible. It's an invitation to try on a new pair of glasses to see things differently. The perspectives I share have turned me into the most vibrant, passionate, and purpose-driven person you'll ever meet. Please note, uncomfortable feelings are likely to arise from the ideas I propose and it's completely normal and expected. I recommend reading this book in phases and stopping to reflect. My conversational tone makes it easy to read, but going slow is likely the best way to digest the perspective.

3. You are exactly where you need to be right this moment. My request: don't compare yourself to others or think you need to be anywhere other than where you are right now. No one taught

us this stuff because they didn't know either. So it does no good to beat yourself up or blame anyone.

4. You are not alone. Maju is a platform for courageous souls to leap hand-in-hand together. We are a community bonded together through a shared vision of thriving on purpose. From transformational live events that will kick your ass into greatness, to in-depth personal growth programs designed to help you cultivate new tools for living well, we are here to support you in truly walking your talk. Find out more online at www.MajuLife.com. If you find you need additional personalized support, please reach out to coach@majulife.com to connect with one of our amazingly talented coaches. We've got your back!

My invitation to you: If you are reading this book, you are likely curious about your potential bubbling under the surface. You may hear a call from within asking you to step up, or perhaps you've come to a place where enough is enough and it's time to make a change. No matter where you are right now, I want you to take the leap. It can be hard, especially when you feel alone. But you are not alone. We all want to feel seen, heard, and loved. We want to know we belong and that others have had similar challenges. We want to accept ourselves and be accepted by others just as we are. Trust me, I get it.

We need models like you in society. We need individuals willing to take responsibility for the energy they are putting out. You are the change agent we've been waiting for. This is the maju way.

Maju... We Evolve On Purpose.

MANIFESTO FOR THRIVING

WE WALK OUR TALK. We are the creators of our experience. *WE PUSH OUR EDGES OF COMFORT IN ORDER TO GROW.*

We believe expressing our authentic self is our greatest asset and the catalyst for personal and societal evolution.

We trust the process. We recognize vulnerability as a strength and an act of courage.

We take risk when our hearts ask us to leap. WE LISTEN DEEPLY. WE ARE FULLY PRESENT.

WE EXPRESS OUR CREATIVITY. WE CHECK OUR ASSUMPTIONS.

WE TAKE PERSONAL RESPONSIBILITY FOR OUR LIVES

We are embodied. We walk through life with humility and curiosity and understand it's our responsibility to evolve into the best version of ourselves in order to thrive. We practice our skills.

WE SHOW UP.

We own our feelings & projections.

WE BELONG. We take care of our mind, body, & soul.

WE LOVE FIERCELY. **We dance. We sing. We live free.**

We are authentic role models for the next generation.

1

THE ROOT CAUSE

There comes an interesting moment in life when time comes to a screeching halt and you look around and question, "How on earth did I get here?" As I stepped off the train and glanced at the six cardboard boxes of my worldly possessions, I could hardly believe I was finally home. I had just spent 10 long years traveling around the country on an unpaved path, only to make a full circle back to where I started.

I moved more times in that decade than most people will in a lifetime. Stability was something I grew up with, yet my curiosity of what else was possible lingered in the forefront of my mind. I recall an inner voice challenging me to stretch myself, despite the overwhelming fear that lived in my body.

My travels revealed more than I could have anticipated about myself and the health of western society. Ten years of new experiences, new faces, and new ideas led to a new awareness of possibilities that kept me on the edge of my seat. Who would I meet next? How would I show up? Would I continue to sabotage my success with old habits, or utilize this transition for growth? My curiosity about what opportunity would come next was exhilarating and terrifying. I repeatedly stepped outside of my comfort zone and tried something new. As a result, I transformed every area of my life. What a ride!

I stepped off the train a very different person. I often wonder what my life would have been like had I not taken those steps to grow. Would I still be struggling with debilitating anxiety, self-hatred, depression, suicidal ideation, and inauthenticity? Would I still feel bottled up, repressed, and controlled by my rambling mind? I use to walk around with a superficial mask, shielding my true feelings from the world. I couldn't keep eye contact for very long because I feared those who were paying attention would see right through me. I watched others dance gracefully through life, expressing themselves freely and I yearned for the day I could do the same. I placed those liberated souls on a pedestal that only amplified my long list of insecurities. I never felt good enough and questioned if I ever would. I couldn't get out of my own damn way.

But how did I even get to that point to begin with?

As a child, I recall dancing like no one was watching. I chewed with my mouth open, finger painted my way to a state of bliss, and spoke whatever random thought popped into my little head. When no one was around, I would act out different movies scenes in front of my mirror dreaming that one day I would become an actress. I rocked leggings with a high waist belt and scrunchy socks like no one's business. I went door to door selling my crappy artwork and hot glued sculptures made of random found objects from the yard. My nails were dirty and my hair was knotty. I was free to be me.

But as I grew older, something happened. Emotional suppression set in. Fear of judgment became an issue. Being authentically seen became scary. I learned right from wrong, good from bad, and praise from scorn. I began to question how others perceived me, caring more about their opinion than my own. I learned how to seek external validation as a means to feel whole inside. When people liked me, I liked myself. When I was criticized, the comments felt like a knife to the heart. I didn't feel good enough, even though I was trying my best with the tools I had.

I came from a very loving family who worked hard day in and day out to provide a better life for me and my siblings. They were warriors in this way, modeling self-discipline and personal responsibility. But as we all know, children are highly susceptible to the world around them. From television shows, school environments, peer groups, babysitters, and even strangers, I learned how to be in this world. But something was off. I wasn't learning how to communicate authentically or love myself just as I am because I had to fit in. I wasn't learning how to be an emotionally intelligent person capable of regulating my own emotions with self-awareness. Instead, I was gathering information about the unspoken social contracts that dictate acceptable ways to behave and react to others. We judge. We blame. We play victim. This is what I saw. I watched my friends get punished for their emotional outbursts, but saw their parents constantly fighting in front of them. I saw the drama on TV and could feel the rush of addicting chemicals flow through my body as if I was getting some kind of fix. I heard the teachers tell us what to think, yet rarely did they encourage us to ask questions and think for ourselves. I learned how to memorize useless information to produce satisfactory test scores so both my school and I could receive praise. As I grew older, I realized how little I was actually taught about how to navigate life with grace.

Growing up as an empathic child I felt the pain, joy, and angst of those around me. It was as if their emotions were my own. I could feel the lull and disappointment people felt in their lives. I experienced their deep desires to do more, but intense fear that stifled their actions. I felt the guilt that lingered in the consciousness of women who had been suppressed by the patriarchal ideals that dominated the previous era. I empathized with the men who were forced to repress their emotions of sadness to conform to the societal gender roles. I was only a child, but I felt the pain of emotional suppression from many generations.

Sleepwalking through life, I realized I was not immune to the same morbid psychology that plagued the consciousness of those who walked before me.

I too had become a product of the unconscious society that damns self-expression and rewards conformity.

Lost in a sea of conformism, how would I ever find my way out? I yearned to express myself authentically again. I craved freedom, choice, and self-acceptance.

I began to wonder where the models of integrity, authenticity, and vulnerability were within our Western culture. Who were we to aspire to in modern day society? My little girl failed to recognize them in the mainstream media or on the latest talk show. That precious little optimist began to lose her way. Her value system was ruled by superficiality and materialism rather than authenticity and personal responsibility.

On a quest to understand, I immersed myself in ethnographies that would give me a glimpse into the life of indigenous cultures. I couldn't understand how modern society had become so disconnected. Part of me burned with curiosity to live among these villages to understand their ways. My lens of the world was limited by my young, sheltered, white privileged bubble and I craved to see more.

When I speak of disconnection, I don't mean proximity or access to each other. I mean authentic connection to our hearts that is then shared with those around us. The songs, dances, and stories shared through the generations of these indigenous cultures peaked my curiosity and the potential for deeper and more meaningful connection. It also amplified my deep desire for wanting more out of my relationships.

But how was I to authentically connect with others when I was so disconnected from myself?

I was longing to feel whole and fulfilled, but no amount of possessions or elevated status could do the trick. What was I missing? How could I be surrounded by people but feel so lonely? Why would my mind race out of control as if on autopilot with a preprogrammed set of reactions?

I was eager for the day I would muster up the courage to make a difference in the world, imagining what it would be like to fully shine without inhibition. I could see the possibility in my mind's eye as if it were already happening, yet my physical reality and old habits were not aligned with the vision I was attempting to manifest.

I had built my psychological framework on faulty premises of who I thought was and what I was capable of achieving.

Underneath this foundation was a rumble of suppressed emotions that became too shaky to ignore. I hid so deep behind my socially acceptable facade that I lost sight of who I was and had become what everyone else wanted me to be. I had been living in a man-made mental prison that society deems as normal. Fear, doubt, and shame were the glue that kept my mask tightly in place. The protective armor wrapped around my body constricted the freedom of authentic and vulnerable expression. Dancing freely and showing the world my true colors was simply not option. I might as well have been locked in a dark chamber hidden from sight.

I carried on in social situations by conforming, not expressing. I scribbled my pain of disconnection across the loose leaf paper that dangled from my college notebook. I screamed for help when no one was around. I numbed myself with socially acceptable drugs that furthered my depression. But no one knew I was depressed. I was too scared to appear less than perfect, yet it was obvious to those around me that I was far from perfect. I was a scared little girl in a growing woman's body, tightly wound and yearning to be loved unconditionally. I was striving to find meaning in life. I was striving to reconnect with my true self.

Who the hell am I and why am I on this planet? What is the meaning of life? Is there a meaning, or am I just as insignificant as the billions of galaxies that littered the sky? These were the questions that lingered in my young mind. I was having an existential crisis that challenged who I thought I was and my entire perception of reality. I could only see the dark cloud that loomed over my head. I was completely lost.

Suppressing my true desire for freedom and creativity would eventually take its toll mentally, emotionally, physically, and spiritually.

I almost killed myself in college because I was too scared and ashamed to be vulnerable and let my imperfect self be seen.

I am not alone on this journey. Too many people silently suffer in a mental prison hiding behind their social mask. We conform to the system and numb our pain, yet yearn to find purpose and self-acceptance. The social contracts that govern our freedom of expression have created an epidemic of emotional suppression that has led to countless suicides, violent acts, and stress-related diseases. This must end now.

Too often we find ourselves staying where we are simply because we don't know what to do next. We repress our emotions thinking no one will understand. We rationalize our problems because we know others around the world struggle more than we ever will. But yet we still feel helpless, alone, and disconnected.

There's a common saying, "You're doing the best you can with the tools you currently have." It turns out, this was the root of my suffering. I lacked critical life skills for quieting my mind, regulating my emotions, and relating authentically.

Acquiring new tools that changed my psychological framework and habitual way of relating to the world was my rope to climb out of the dark well of sorrow. I had to truly surrender and open my mind to new ideas.

The lens through which I viewed the world had become so fogged up that I forgot my perception was just one way of seeing things.

This is what the Maju Mindset is all about. We must surrender our attachment to our outdated perceptual lenses and reconfigure our view to include new possibilities. Otherwise, we will continue to see the same results and sacrifice our true happiness.

TURNING POINT

So how does one make a turning point in their life when all hope is lost? When there is no inner validation, self-love, or tools to cope? How do you pull yourself out of the dark well when no one knows you're down there?

Despite my insatiable outward focus, I heard a whisper from deep within that said, "Don't settle. There's a better way. Remember who you are." The churning sensation that burned in my chest was unmistakable. It was as if there was a violet flame dancing in my heart, illuminating a potential path forward, and echoing the voice that was attempting to speak through me. But the voice wasn't coming from my mind. It was coming from my heart. It was soothing, validating, and trustworthy. It told me to take back my power and rise up. It told me I would be safe and supported. Yet my physiological response of fear was far too debilitating to take action. I knew there had to be a different way to live, but how would I cultivate the courage to take the leap into the dark holding onto just a thread of intuition? I had been hardwired to avoid doing exactly that. I was led to believe I was powerless and stuff just happened to me. Lingering in despair was no longer an option. I had to choose something different. I had to believe in possibilities.

The first ray of light that pierced the walls of my morbid state came with the realization that I didn't have to be controlled by my rambling mind. I had the power to let go of my thoughts, relax my body, and release my stress. The little optimist within was buried so deep that a shred of light was like the heavens opening up. I could feel my heart, vulnerable and in pain, wanting to accept this to be true. But I was still scared. I read countless case studies about the neuroscience of mindfulness as a means to soothe my analytical mind. The deeper I plunged into other people's experience of transformation the more courage I had to take the leap myself.

MEDITATION Y'ALL

Exploring meditation is like tasting an exotic food for the first time. Your first impression may be laced with unsubstantiated judgments. You may assume it's not right for you, until you finally cave in to curiosity. The first bite is coated with preconceived expectations that shade your perception. The second bite, if you are courageous enough to continue, gives you a better sense of what it actually tastes like. Eventually you acquire the palate for such an experience. This is the art of learning meditation. Once you get a real taste for the practice, you can't believe you ever lived without it. The same is true for beer and bourbon.

This fascinated me. Making small steps toward improvement, I decided to dive deeper into my studies. I had to road test the plethora of techniques for myself. Could all this shit really work? I became engulfed in practices that challenged me to be vulnerable while remaining present in the moment and owning my feelings. I took the time to meditate each day and journal about what I noticed. In a short amount of time, everything began to change. The dark cloud that lingered above my head for so long seemed to be fading from sight. I was no longer attached to the morbid ideas I use to believe as my truths. The fake mask I wore began to dissolve as I realized I didn't give a flying fuck what other people thought of me. If they judge me, that's their stuff. I was finally being true to me and learning that I was good enough just as I am. The sky was turning blue again.

How come I had never heard the inner whisper before? Was it because there were no pauses between my thoughts? Why didn't anyone teach me this? Once I released my inner child's frustration with a system that hadn't bothered to teach me this basic life skill, I discovered compassion like I had never experienced it before. It wasn't that people didn't care, they just didn't know. They were skeptical and had formed strong opinions before ever tasting the goods for themselves. Surely they would have shared this wisdom with me had they truly known.

I had reached my breaking point and the walls of resistance came tumbling down. It was now up to me to rework my inner world, one moment at a time.

Humbled by the process, I surrendered my shield and set off on a decade long journey traveling across the country, diving off cliffs of uncertainty to see what else I might be missing (the full details of that decade's journey is a book within itself – coming soon to a bookstore near you). Once I had a taste, I had to know what else was possible. Could I actually be limitless if I was willing to continually lean into my edge of discomfort? Could the crazy ideas from my heart and the images in my mind actually mean something? My conclusion: Hell yeah!

My insatiable curiosity about psychology, interpersonal neurobiology, spirituality, and the human condition consumed me for over a decade and impacted every decision I made. There was no turning back. I learned the power of leaping into the unknown and could call bullshit on my own stories, knowing that personal liberation was on the other side. I was having a spiritual awakening and everything was changing.

The key is knowing thyself and trusting the whisper that echoes within the stillness.

The more I dove into the depths of myself and chose to let go of the layers of social programming and limiting perceptions, the more I become aware that something else was at play. I was no longer a helpless victim to circumstance. I became consciously engaged with the creation of reality and learned I have power over my response to life. Knowing myself, beyond just who and what I thought I was, turned out to be the key to cultivating a soul satisfying life and truly having an impact on this planet.

Stepping off that train was like completing a victory lap for my soul. I am not the same person I use to be. Not even close. I no longer struggle with debilitating social anxiety, a lack of self-confidence, depression, suicidal ideation, inauthenticity, and an overwhelming fear of failure. I am now liberated in my own self-expression because I learned how to get out of my own damn way. I trust my intuition without reservation and love myself unconditionally. I leap when my heart guides me and I probably smile more than anyone you'll ever meet. I am consciously engaged with the creation of my reality and know I have more power over my responses, even when I'm triggered. I make shit happen because I choose to.

I find it fascinating and quite humbling that the people I encounter today are hard pressed to believe that I could have ever been any different. All they see is the passionate and outspoken woman who has found peace within herself and isn't afraid to challenge the status quo (something I use to be terrified of). I chose to take action and rework my perception. I spent time getting to know the many facets of myself, completely altering my view of reality and sense of freedom. Trust me when I say, if I can transform as much as I have, you can too.

My journey continues to dramatically morph as I become even more steady on my solid foundation of inner trust, authenticity, and creative self-expression. My heart is alive and guiding each and every step I take – as an entrepreneur, traveler, writer, speaker, daughter, friend, and lover.

I dance. I sing. I live free. And so will you.

Standing in the Shadow
By Kristi Lee Schatz

We see outside but not within
Projecting the past of where we have been.
Stuck in our minds and out of our hearts
The world we see is through our own dark.
Those shadows that plague our vision and sight
Keep us creating the same night after night after night.

Do you believe what you see in the world to be true?
Or do you foster ideas that could bring anew?
A new awareness and perception of our limitless nature
That nurtures the spirit of the creative maker.
The part within that seems to know
That moves and shakes to help you grow.
Conditioned to believe that we need to be
Separate from you and isolated to me,
Yet sharing in truth is what will set us free
Because in essence you are not really separate from me.
Duality is an illusion of our limited selves
Blinded by our judgment of everyone else.
Those shadows that plague our vision and sight
Keep us creating the same night after night after night.

But what if you could surrender and let it all go
Releasing your fears and concerns of the status quo?
The social contracts that govern who you should be
How you should express, and define you as separate from me.
Push against the edge of what you believe
And you'll redefine what you can achieve.
Settling on less would be a detriment to your soul
For your true essence has but one goal.
To live and love without inhibition
And bring your dreams into fruition.

Your creative self yearns to re-emerge
Because it observes that you're on the verge.
The verge of remembering and restoring that which is true
The Divine awakening that will help you see through.
Beyond the illusion of isolation
And into the awareness of your incarnation.
Gone are the days of projection and disconnection
As we realize that love is the only pure reflection.
Reflection of our beauty and our light
Is the gas that fuels the flame to ignite.
If growing and glowing is the path of true knowing
Then we shall burn bright to keep it all flowing.

Those shadows that plague our vision and sight
Cannot sustain in the wake of our light,
As the truth exposes the falsehoods of our fright
And crumbles the walls that held us so tight.
Bound, constricted and silenced no more
We will rise to remember our infinite core.
Knowing our being is absolutely pure
Will free us from our cycle of this human chore.
You are the maker and that is true
Everything you see exists within the depths you.
Choosing freedom over comfort will bring anew
For awakening the spirit is not reserved for a few.
Your heart is alive and aware of more
Waiting for you to connect and find out for sure.
Step aside and end the chase
For your destination is already in place.
The silence is a means to create the space
Which opens the door to reveal your grace.
Those shadows that plagued your vision and sight
Can no longer remain in the wake of your unbound and
Illuminated light.

Be yourself, free yourself, love yourself, and rise
For the time has come for you to open your eyes.

2

F#%K THE RULES
(WITH GRACE)

People are ready for realness. We are tired of doing the same old thing. We want to express our authentic selves and let go of our facades. We don't want our children to grow up in a world riddled by fear, judgment, and hatred. We are ready to brace our unrealized potential. We are ready to thrive.

It only takes one individual to step out of the box of current thinking and do something different for the world to change. Will you be that person in society? Will you be that parent for your child?

It is apparent that most adults are tightly wound creatures busting at the seams, yearning for freedom of expression and authenticity, yet fearful of the vulnerability of being imperfect and judged. We are not taught the importance of self-love and acceptance. We hold in our emotions and project unrealistic expectations onto others. We absorb the identity of what others expect us to be and we play our societal roles to a T. But at what cost?

Are you genuinely happy, healthy, and creating a vibrant life? Are you painting the world with your unique color, or are you blending in for fear of standing out? Are you holding yourself back because you don't feel like you have permission to express yourself?

In our subconscious minds, hidden from sight, lays a rulebook for how to navigate life. Beyond the rules governed by moral and ethical perspectives are rules about appropriate self-expression. These include how you communicate your feelings, the comfort zones you adhere to, and the expectations you hold for yourself and others. The question is, did you consciously create the rules, or are you playing by someone else's rules? Do you even know what's in your rulebook?

Were you reprimanded for speaking your truth? Were you told to hold in your emotions and suck it up? Did you learn it's not safe to step outside the box and be different because people will judge you? Or, did you learn vicariously by watching others get in trouble for their expressions and decide not to repeat the same mistake? No matter what you learned about how to be in this world, it's your responsibility to ensure it's truly what you want for your own life.

The quality of your life is determined by the content of your inner world. Whether you are aware of it or not, you are expressing who and what you have learned to be. What you don't accept about yourself, you don't accept in others. These social rules become your perceptual lens through which you see the world and dictate your reactions and judgments of others. These are the glasses we pass down to our children.

The Maju Mindset is a perspective on life. It's a way to see the world through a lens that is both self-aware and socially engaged, thus deepening your sense of aliveness and intimacy. When you are blinded by the perceptual lenses and rules passed down by others, it's easy to become unconsciously reactive to your environment and unaware of how your presence is impacting the quality of your relationships. Shifting the way you view yourself and the world around you is a critical step in creating a new landscape to play in.

The voice of society and the opinion of others are like an audio tape on replay in our minds, drowning out the whisper from within asking us to take that step and stand tall. Our self-sabotaging habits keep us from living up to our full potential, despite our insatiable desire to feel more whole and alive. We play small and hide behind the limiting stories of our minds because we are too afraid of doing something different. We are ashamed of being vulnerable and letting the world see all the stuff we stored away for a rainy day. It doesn't help that the voice of society tells us to hide certain parts of ourselves for fear of being judged and looking crazy. But here's the issue: What we push down and try to avoid is energy lodged in our body, vibrating for the world to feel. This is the heavy weight we carry around. No matter how much we try to hide or avoid it, it's always there waiting for the day we will be brave enough to acknowledge it. As long as we remain chained to our old way of being and unconsciously play into the social agreements that restrict vulnerable and authentic self-expression, we will struggle to move forward.

We are all perpetuating this dysfunctional cycle by hiding ourselves and judging others.

How will we ever create a deeply connected world that values diversity and empowers each person to shine their unique light if we don't even recognize the light within ourselves? How will we inspire the next generation to live extraordinary lives if we keep doing what hasn't been working? There must be another way to function as a society. There must be a way for us to thrive together.

GET OUT OF YOUR BOX

The mental, emotional, and physical walls that box you into your present reality are likely constructed by an outdated rulebook and have little to do with who you really are. Tapping into your true self is like turning on the light in a dark hallway because it illuminates the false walls that keep you feeling trapped. Defining yourself by your past experiences is like buying into the illusion that you are forever stuck in that hallway. You are not. The walls will crumble once you believe you are no longer limited by the obstacles that stand in front of you. How bright can you really be if you're stuck behind four walls?

Stepping out of your own way so your full self may express freely requires you to shift your perception of what is possible and let go of your resistance to being vulnerable. Yes, it's scary. I totally get that. But so is the reality of feeling trapped within yourself for the remainder of your days on earth. Would you rather feel uncomfortable emotions from time to time and grow from the experience, or live a life filled with regret from missed opportunities and the heavy weight of unprocessed emotions? You have more potential than your mind will allow you to fathom and the Maju Mindset is an opportunity to take hold of the viewfinder and essentially say, "fuck the rules, this is my life." Your kids will thank you for this gift you give to yourself.

The unseen power that lies behind the chatter of your rambling mind is waiting for you to tune in, listen without expectation, and take action when needed. This is when miracles occur. As you blow on the flame that resides within, it illuminates the fallacies of your subconscious mind and restores the power to make the changes you seek in your life.

We are all products of our journey. Some find strength to overcome the monumental challenges that stand in their way, while others are hardened or weakened by life's weathering. We haven't learned about compassion, forgiveness, mindfulness, projection, unconditional love, trust, authenticity, or vulnerability. That obvious by the state of affairs around the world and surely isn't an aspect of the public education system in the Western world. We're all bruised in some way by our experiences. This is what makes us human. Our shared experiences of pain, triumph, and victory no matter how big or small are the threads that bond us in our human condition. Learning to show the real, raw, and vulnerable parts of ourselves is the path to creating more intimacy in relationships. We can finally see that we're not that different after all. If we remove our façade of perfection to let the authentic self shine, it significantly increases our sense of confidence in who we really are. Otherwise, we walk around meeting strangers over and over again, until one of us is ready to be real and let the other person in. We project onto successful people, placing them on a pedestal and minimize our success along the way. How the hell is this helping anyone? The rules are the glue binding us to our perpetual loneliness and a sense of disconnection.

Life boils down to a series of choices. You can take personal responsibility for the quality of your inner world knowing it creates your experiences, or you can play victim to circumstance. You can express yourself authentically leaving your unique mark on this world, or hide behind your socially acceptable mask which dims your light. You can step outside of your comfort zone and be vulnerable in order to grow, or stay exactly where you are. You can learn to trust the process of life as it unfolds knowing your hardships are lessons, or you can continue to feel as if nothing ever goes your way. You can choose to fine tune the quality of your presence and be a role model to the next generation, or you can live in reaction to your environment and unconsciously pass along your social rulebook to our children. It's really up to you.

Our reactions based on past programming are the stones in the road we tend to trip over. We repeat the same patterns expecting different results until life comes along and gives us new tools to build a more solid foundation. But this doesn't have to be the only way. Gaining wisdom from the hard knocks of life is an old way of evolving. Choosing to take steps each day to explore your inner world without judgment, listening to the quality of your self-talk with curiosity, and training your brain to be still in the present moment will exponentially increase your level of self-awareness and make lasting changes in the way you show up in the world. This is the maju way to approach life (or as my team calls it, Maju Style!)

Within you lies all of the answers you'll ever need along with the power to heal and transform your entire life.

Hitting your breaking point simply means a new horizon is about to open, but only if you choose to seize the opportunity. Discovering who you really are and reconstructing your life to live in alignment is one of the most rewarding, yet challenging missions we can embark on as humans.

I have interviewed countless people to figure out the catalyst for their downward spiral and learned it has less to do with their worth or capacity for success and more to do with a lack of tools to efficiently process their own emotions. Maybe deep down inside you there is a dormant seed waiting to be watered by the light of a new perspective. Maybe others have this seed too, yearning for someone to reflect the possibility for growth and transformation.

At some point, all seedlings must break free from the shell that holds them back in order to grow. I hit my emotional breaking point at a young age as a result of the destructive stories I created about my self-worth and my habit of repressing my emotions. I could sense there was sunlight above the ground covering my shell and desired to break free and blossom.

I was forced to tear down the walls of negative perceptions to consciously rework the foundation of my life. I had to let go of the opinions and expectations of others and learn how to take back my power so that I could create the life I truly wanted. I was not a victim of my world, but an active participant with new opportunities to thrive each and every day. I had to disengage from the push-pull battle of needing to be understood and simply be OK with the fact that I am different.

But let me be real here. It was hard as hell to get to this place because I always felt alone and didn't fully understand how to surrender. I thought I should be farther along than I was and constantly compared myself to others who were flourishing. It wasn't until I realized I am exactly where I am supposed to be and learned to trust the process as it is that I finally broke free from having to work so hard. I'm not supposed to be like anyone else. Sure, I admire many people for their badassery, but once I started to love myself just as I am, I discovered I'm kind of a badass too. Who knew?

No matter who you are and what life you have lived, at your core you are good enough and deserve love. The choices you have made and actions you have taken are yours to own. But they do not define who you are and what you are capable of. You are not your thoughts, cultural conditioning, past experiences, or even your self-identified personality. The real you is the observer behind the scenes. You are a light flickering from the flame that is yearning to be fanned. As soon as you begin to embrace yourself as a magnificent, creative, and universal force of energy you will have the ability to transcend all barriers and obstacles. When you open yourself to receiving more love, abundance, and happiness, you begin to receive more of the same. So why would you want to continue functioning as if you have no control? You are an alchemist. Own it.

LET'S TALK AWARENESS

The Maju Mindset is all about awareness. I see when I fucked up. I catch myself when I'm triggered. I notice when I'm hiding my truths. I acknowledge when I'm taking life too seriously, and I recognize others are not responsible for my feelings. The process that unfolds once you've been brave enough to shine a light on yourself is pure magic and deserves a double high five, Maju Style. Seriously, our inner child is begging to play more. We must celebrate our successes, even when we make the slightest progress forward, because it feeds the soul of the hungry little one within. Plus it feels great and inoculates our cells with a neurochemical cocktail that elevates our energy and mood. It's a win-win folks.

Tackling life without self-awareness can feel like being blindfolded on a battlefield. It leads to poor decisions, repeated failures and no integration of the important lessons. To have never explored the inner depths of our psyche is to function in a chaotic world, unwittingly contributing to the chaos. I imagine the majority of us seek to dance through life, yet many of us are blinded by our psychological conditioning or lost in a daydream. Reactive behavior stemming from a lack of self and social awareness increases stress and impacts our wellbeing. Learning to effectively identify and regulate emotions from a place of self-awareness can help to foster a sense of inner balance and influence the quality of interpersonal relationships

Self-awareness also transforms your relationship with yourself by dissolving the falsehoods your mind holds as absolutes. These are the walls that barricade you into a small space, suffocating your greatness. When you learn to accept yourself just as you are and recognize that your mental pictures are illusions, you will find the courage to unzip your emotional coat and rework the story of your life. Would you have consciously chosen to live in a small box if the potential for being limitless was modeled to you from an early age? Of course not. The system is broken, not you.

ASSUMPTIONS ARE SO LAST YEAR

Everyone's path is going to look different. When we assume we know the best path for someone we are doing them a great disservice of figuring it out for themselves. We inflict our expectations on them and project disappointments when they stray. I wandered on roads less traveled but it didn't mean I was lost. The opposite actually. For the first time in my life I was beginning to listen to my true self and it looked different from the traditional path. I made mistakes along the way and failed countless times. The worse thing that happened was personal growth. It's all a matter of perspective.

Assuming you know what another person is thinking or feeling is like shoving them into your bubble of reality without checking to see if they actually want to be there. Simply checking your assumptions from a space of curiosity and honesty is a great way to get to know the inner workings of another person and adds depth to the quality of your connection.

The Maju Mindset is a perceptual shift that, when applied regularly and consciously, develops a deeper understanding of yourself and others. That seems pretty critical if we're going to create a more connected planet for our children to thrive in.

Let's talk about our children for a moment. We think children are incapable of comprehending complex ideas like the nature of reality. That's bullshit. They are extremely intuitive little creatures that figure it out by relying on cues from their environment. Their senses are beyond what we are tuned into as adults because they aren't yet numbed, hardened, and weathered by the experiences of life. They are open, vulnerable, and trusting that the world will show them the way. But we aren't.

Children spend up to 14,040 hours in grade school. This makes it a great platform for teaching skill sets that increase emotional intelligence and mindfulness. Every child's home life is different - some extremely stressful, others peaceful. Having an education system that focuses on building a child's ability to regulate their emotions and find inner peace can have a dramatic effect on their ability to learn and grow. Rather than shaming them through harsh punishment, why don't we take the time to actually teach them the skills to overcome their inner challenges? Every child deserves the same opportunity to excel in life, no matter what their socio-economic status is. We must use the education system as a neutral playing field that brings our children together through compassion and understanding. But it all starts with adults having the awareness that something else is possible and having the courage to take action. It's important to remember that each student, teacher, and administrator has a different rulebook, all projected on each other. But what if we just had five rules?

1. We take personal responsibility for our feelings and projections in the moment as they arise to make us aware of our possible reactive behavior.

2. We have permission to show up authentically and so do others.

3. We express ourselves when we feel vulnerable and don't fear judgment from others because if they choose to judge, that's their shit.

4. We trust that, even in turmoil, there is a lesson to be learned if we're paying attention.

5. We show up as unconditionally loving role models capable of setting healthy boundaries while respecting individual self-expression.

I truly believe life would have been easier to navigate had these rules been planted into my young mind. I know we are capable of breaking this cycle for the next generation if we collectively choose to.

As you journey through this book, just remember: life is an art form. It takes time and regular practice to master your craft. Learning acceptance, patience, and trust can help you live more fully, but those qualities aren't developed overnight.

The art of living well requires you to consciously take full responsibility for the life you're creating. You hold the paintbrush and the blueprint. From your inner dialogue to your lifestyle choices, you're truly in control of every stroke on the canvas of life.

Beyond the layers of habit and learned responses is a masterful artist. Uncovering this creative potential requires your willingness to explore and adjust each stroke, or choice, moment to moment.

Taking time to quiet your racing thoughts, adjust your self-talk, and fine tune your actions to align with your goals are all paths toward harnessing the artist within. To master this delicate art form, you must recognize that you're the only one who can make these choices and accept that you're entirely capable of personal transformation.

Approaching life as a creative canvas will free you from the psychology of helplessness and place the power of the paintbrush back in your hands. The art is in trusting that each stroke actively brings you closer to the peace and freedom you desire. But you must first choose to pick up the brush and make a stroke. Joining your local fitness club, learning meditation, attending a personal development seminar, or even challenging yourself to run a marathon are all paths that could lead to a greater sense of health and happiness. Since no two artists are the same, everyone will walk a unique path toward awakening their inner master. Watching how each person chooses to show up in the world makes this art form as interesting as witnessing a fine artist creating a masterpiece right before our eyes.

But a word of caution: while overcoming life's hurdles can be invigorating, we must be careful not to hide behind rose-colored glasses and escape to utopia. This art form is to be mastered through life's ebbs and flows. That includes rush hour traffic delays, fussy children at the supermarket, or a lack of time to complete all your chores and errands.

The art is in the response.

These are opportunities to practice your new skills and surrender to what you can't control. Just as a painter chooses to use magenta rather than sky blue, you too can choose the shade, intensity, and depth of your mental, emotional, and behavioral response.

It's also important to remember that each person's health and happiness matters in the greater scheme of things. Just as you have the power to create a masterpiece for yourself, your efforts influence the greater whole that makes up this global mosaic. Your unique expression and participation in the world is a key ingredient in creating a luscious and vibrant landscape for us all to enjoy.

The key is conscious choice and action. You must choose to explore and participate in all that life has to offer. Otherwise, your potential for truly living well will remain locked within your present comfort zone.

Your shade of pink may be different than your neighbor's and that's perfectly OK. It's diversity that creates our magical and vibrant landscape, and it will continue to evolve as each person steps forward, takes hold of the paintbrush, and consciously leaves their unique mark on this world. Stroke by stroke, you are painting this thing called life. Be diligent, be mindful, and have fun!

Choosing to Shine
By Kristi Lee Schatz

Be careful what you feed your mind, it will affect your body.
Be careful what you feed your body, it will affect your mind.

See, you are not separate beings functioning without cause
Every action you take might make others pause.
Pause to think, reflect, and even shift the way they behave.

Why we choose to function without awareness is insane
For walking blindfolded on this earth is a recipe for pain.

How you treat others is a reflection of yourself
Your judgments, insecurities, and banter impact your health.
Projecting your box of reality onto others expecting them to comply
Removes you from the vibration of love and into a world you try to deny.

Choosing love over hate is a choice only you can make.
Love for yourself, others, and all life on this planet is what I postulate.
Living and loving freely to your fullest is the greatest gift you can give
For you model to the next generation the best way to live.

We must rise and stand together
We must shine our light and make this world better.
There is no more room for hiding, ignoring, or pretending
Ours children's future depends on us defending.
Defending the rights of all living beings
And standing in unison for all things unseen.

Our small programmed minds can't possibly know the truth for sure but
our open hearts can leads us down a path that might reveal the real cure.

See vulnerability is the way
As it removes barricades that keep you from experiencing
your greatest day.
When you shut the world out, you shut yourself in
Causing you much pain because your light is dim.

If we want a revolution of light on this earth
It will not come from hatred, judgment, or our own hurt.
It will come from the stillness that resides within
That place of awareness, compassion, and forgiveness of our sins.

It will emerge from the depths of our souls
Illuminating our unconscious and taking us off cruise control.

It's up to you to be the best you can be
And not beat yourself up for what you cannot see.
Make each moment an opportunity to evolve
And realize that you are a conditioned human
And that you will fall.

Your life is a chance to learn, grow, and explore
I just ask that you also choose to shine more.

As you nurture the seedling of possibility from within
You will find yourself blossoming and smiling with a grin.
For you have awoken to your grand potential and the impact
You can have on the world will be monumental.

The time has come to rise and shine
And let yourself merge with all that is Divine.

Maju Style

What if you had a pair of high-tech, invisible glasses that could alter your view of reality? Imagine if you could instantly shift your perception from judgment to curiosity and remember to not take life too seriously. Welcome to the Maju Mindset.

> A New Lens of Reality

3

THE MAJU MINDSET

The Maju Mindset is like a new pair of really cool glasses that turn fog into sunlight. The lenses are coated with five principles, or perspectives, that immediately shift your attention from habitual reaction to inquisitive self-exploration. When you sport your new specs, it's easier to let the small stuff go and return to the present moment with a genuine sense of curiosity. Pretty high tech stuff!

These glasses represent a mindset that encompasses a few very important principles that were left out of modern day education. Each component is equally important on its own, but when combined the transformation can be unprecedented. These principles are not just conceptual ideas, but states of awareness that deepen throughout the course of a lifetime. They are seeds planted in the conscious mind that bring to light the contradictory logic of your subconscious programming. The more you water them with your attention and time, the greater they flourish into buds of possibility.

Over time, the light within will grow brighter allowing your radiant self to blossom. In the words of James Redfield, "Where attention goes, energy flows…" You reap what you sow.

The process of integrating the principles will look different for everyone and there is no right way to step on this path. You simply have to believe another way is possible and allow these principles to guide you along your journey through deeper self-inquiry. Each moment is an opportunity to adjust the lens of reality to include these principles as a possible way of relating to yourself and the world around you. When you're feeling stuck, pull out your metaphorical glasses, acknowledge how cool you look, and proceed to explore the situation at hand without judgment. Or better yet, simply say, "It's time to get my maju on!"

Layer by layer, you will peel away the old self-concepts that had become your identity. You begin to see the world through a clearer lens and create opportunities that were once only a faint idea. You gain insight into the limitless nature of your being, develop compassion for those around you and erase the emotional triggers that once ruled your life. If you allow yourself to be authentic, accept your vulnerability, trust the process and own your feelings and projections, you will not only transform your life, but role model the possibilities to those you encounter. While some people might not understand and even judge you (despite how cool you look in your epic new glasses), the practice is to surrender and be true to yourself no matter the circumstance. In time, as the quality of your life dramatically improves, people will start asking questions about what's working so well for you. Remember, it's not your job to change anyone. Just be present to yourself and evolve on purpose. You are not better than anyone else, nor is anyone better than you. This isn't about spiritualizing the ego, or bypassing our uncomfortable feelings. It's about being present to what is alive within you and shining light on the principles to reveal deeper layers of yourself. This is the type of world I want for my future children and I invite you to co-create it with me. These are the five principles of the Maju Mindset:

1. Personal Responsibility
2. Authenticity
3. Vulnerability
4. Trust
5. Role Modeling

Let's break these down a little...

1. Personal Responsibility: We are the creators of our experience. We thrive because we are willing to take ownership of the quality of our inner world and outward responses. We do not play victim because we ultimately know we are in the driver's seat. We choose to take responsibility for our feelings and check our assumptions to break the cycle of projection and disconnection for the betterment of the planet as a whole.

2. Authenticity: We believe expressing our authentic self is our greatest asset and the catalyst for personal and societal evolution. We recognize our differences and celebrate our diversity. We don't hide our feelings and we speak from a space of personal ownership to deepen our connection and intimacy with others.

3. Vulnerability: We recognize vulnerability as a strength and an act of courage. We take risks when our heart asks us to leap and we push our edge of discomfort in order to grow. We vulnerably share our imperfections with others because we know we're all on this human journey together and no one is perfect. We know that holding in our emotions creates walls in our minds and tension in our bodies and we refuse to create more suffering for ourselves.

4. Trust: We trust the process of growth and transformation and we trust our hearts implicitly. When the whisper speaks through the stillness we listen and integrate the guidance to shift our perceptual lens of possibilities. We don't fight life as it happens, we flow through it, learning and growing along the way. We trust that there is no such thing as failure, just opportunities to practice.

5. Role Modeling: We walk our talk and embody our practice. We fully show up as the expression we wish to see flourish in the world. As we develop ourselves, we share our humble and vulnerable lessons for the wellbeing of the next generation. We know our unconditionally loving and non-judgmental presence will instill a healthy sense of freedom around self-expression for the children of this world and everyone we touch.

So why these five principles? You'll soon discover that these five elements encompass pretty much every area of our lives.

Over and over again, these principles continued to show up in my life. At every transition, life challenge, and opportunity they would appear like guide posts for deeper self-inquiry. Am I willing to take personal responsibly for how I just reacted to that circumstance? Can I let myself be authentic in this meeting, or will I keep hiding? Am I willing to unzip my emotional coat and be vulnerable in this moment despite the fear I feel in my body? Am I willing to have a new experience and step outside of my comfort zone? Can I truly trust the universe has my back and let go of the push-pull of trying to figure everything out? Am I really showing up in the world and role modeling that which I wish to see flourish? Every circumstance brought up a different set of questions and responses, but the five guiding principles remained the same. All I had to do was put on the glasses and the deeper truth revealed itself.

For most of my journey, no matter how I framed the questions, the answers to the five principles were a resounding no. And you know what? I was depressed, anxious, and always felt like a helpless victim. My mind would try to trick me into believing I could say yes from time to time, but my deeper truth knew that was bullshit.

I didn't understand the importance of evolving myself on purpose. I thought life just happened. I didn't realize how much my perception and lack of action perpetuated my discontentment. I didn't know and that's OK because it's the journey through the principles that matters, not the destination.

Let's face it, we're all human. We're going to screw up from time to time. It's fine. The point is to take a deep breath, try not to beat yourself up too much, and take your next step forward. When you fall again, go back to the principles and get real with yourself. Then choose to step forward once more.

Some challenges are easier to overcome than others depending upon the meaning you attach to them. Let that be OK. Each experience will unfold and reveal deeper parts of yourself so long as you're present and curious. The more you learn about your inner world, the greater your self-awareness. This can lead to a pivotal shift in your life.

The following chapters outline the five principles in depth. At the end of each chapter I share a short interview with someone who has impacted my life and get their take on what the principle means to them. Multiple perspectives are key! In addition, I've included a few fun "play dates" for you to dive deeper into yourself immediately. My advice: don't skip over the exercises. You must do the work to see the results.

Let's get this party started!

Life is a Metaphor
By Kristi Lee Schatz

I write to express. I write to know.
I write to dissolve the falsehood of perceptions in order to grow.

As I wander through metaphor, climbing mountains and
Roaming dark forest, I begin to see.
I see the light of day, the sunset into the darkness of fear
The clouds that linger from past ideas, and the water moving
Ever so steady in the meadow of the frontier.

I see the world hidden from sight
As I jump down the rabbit hole of perceptual fright.
Hanging on to a thread of trust
I plunge deep into the sea of shadows knowing I must.

I must awaken to the whisper.
I must follow the voice that echos from the inner cave
Reverberating a call off the walls of doubt and blame.

I must explore to sense what is alive
For standing still will keep me obliged
To the self concepts that continue to blanket my eyes
And silence my voice to keep me disguised.

Hidden from sight, away from the world
My true self stays armored and furled.

But the ground will shake and the walls will fall
Leaving me open, vulnerable and exposed to all.

No matter the grip I try to hold
The process will inevitably unfold.
Until I surrender and let it just be
For that is the moment I discover the real me.

I write to see. I write to know.
I write to uncover the truth which is still to be told.

Maju Style

If the mirror is foggy, wipe the damn thing off. Unless you like the distorted reflection of yourself, then by all means, keep it up!

> Personal Responsibility

4

PRINCIPLE 1: PERSONAL RESPONSIBILITY

The latest research in neuroscience and epigenetics depicts a fascinating tale of how our experiences and environments create our reality and alter our biology. The stories we play in our minds create neurological loops that keep us seeing reality through the lens of the past. Our emotional connection and perception of an experience creates a concoction of neurochemicals that flood our cells with information about how to respond to a situation physiologically.

When you shift your emotional relationship and narrative of the story, you change which chemical messengers are delivered to your cells and thus engage in a biological reprogramming process. Changing your story reshapes your brain's neurological structure because you are actively choosing to be in the present moment, rather than lost in an old way of seeing the world.

The following excerpt is from "Power of the Mind in Health and Healing" by Keith R. Holden, M.D. Holden is a physician who is board certified in Internal Medicine and trained in Functional Medicine. He has graciously contributed his research findings and insights to the Maju Mindset to help explain some of the science that supports the mind-body connection. If you're interested in exploring more about the scientific research and Holden's unique perspective on health and healing, then check out his book. He is an extraordinary human being who takes personal responsibility to a whole new level.

MIND-BODY GENOMICS

Mind-body genomics is the study of how your mind influences your genes to turn on and off. This field of study is in its infancy, but early research is producing some amazing results. By practicing mindfulness and meditation, you learn to regulate your thoughts. By regulating your thoughts, you can trigger your relaxation response. The relaxation response causes genes to turn on and off that optimize your health. A study co-authored by Dr. Herbert Benson in 2013 shows how this happens.[1]

Dr. Benson is a medical doctor and one of the founding fathers of mind-body medicine. He coined the term "relaxation response" almost forty years ago. He says the relaxation response is the opposite of the stress response, and is induced by any mind-body practice that produces relaxation. Dr. Benson set out to study if the relaxation response turned genes on and off. Participants in this study included inexperienced and experienced practitioners of the relaxation response.

Both groups completed eight weekly training sessions. In these training sessions, they learned a relaxation technique, diaphragmatic breathing, body scanning, mantra repetition, and mindfulness meditation. They also listened to a 20-minute audio track guiding them through the same sequence at home once a day. Researchers analyzed gene expression in participants at the beginning and at the end of the study and here is what they found.

The relaxation response turns on genes involved in the production of energy by mitochondria, which are the batteries of the cell. The relaxation response suppresses inflammation and turns on genes that dampen oxidative stress. This is analogous to reducing body rust. The relaxation response turns on genes increasing insulin production, which has the potential to result in better blood sugar regulation. The relaxation response also has an anti-aging effect, in that it preserves the ends of your chromosomes called telomeres. Not surprisingly, all these beneficial effects were more pronounced in the experienced practitioners.

MEDITATION IS ANTI-INFLAMMATORY

Science shows that mindfulness and meditation turn genes on and off to reduce inflammation. Because excessive inflammation causes disease, a reduction in excessive inflammation translates into health benefits. A study published in 2014 shows that the anti-inflammatory effect of mindfulness happens quite rapidly.[2] In this study, a group of expert meditators underwent eight hours of intensive mindfulness.

Researchers performed a gene analysis comparing the expert meditators to a control group who underwent eight hours of quiet non-meditative activities. What they found was that an intensive day of mindfulness in expert meditators is a powerful anti-inflammatory. It triggered the same gene pathway as the anti-inflammatory drug Celebrex, but without the side effects.

The body creates inflammation through several genetic pathways. One involves a cell protein called nuclear factor kappa B (NFKB). Multiple studies show that mindfulness meditation reduces inflammation by turning off NFKB.[3,4,5,6]

By using mindfulness and meditation to reduce stressful thoughts, you trigger a relaxation response. This relaxation response has a positive influence on how your genes turn on and off, or how they express. So by learning to manipulate your thoughts, you indirectly affect how your genes express. It turns out you can also manipulate your thoughts to grow new neuronal pathways in your brain. Some call this self-directed neuroplasticity.

SELF-DIRECTED NEUROPLASTICITY

Neuroplasticity is your brain's ability to physically change and adapt. We used to think that neuroplasticity only occurred in early childhood. We now know that the adult brain is capable of creating new neuronal pathways. Your environment and your actions influence your brain's ability to create new neuronal pathways. This requires a sustained change in your pattern of neural activity. For your brain to create new neuronal pathways, you need to do something in a repetitive manner to create long-lasting changes.

An example of neuroplasticity is what occurs when someone undergoes rehabilitation after a stroke. Rehabilitation to recover neurologic function forces the brain to create new neuronal pathways. These new pathways take over function for the areas of the brain injured by the stroke.

Self-directed neuroplasticity is the ability to create new neuronal connections in your brain through regular mindfulness and meditation. Here's an example. In 2005, researchers imaged the brains of experienced meditators. They found that long-term meditation produces neuroplastic effects. It thickens areas of the brain associated with attention, interoception, and sensory processing.[7] Interoception is your awareness of your body's internal regulation.

These findings were more pronounced in older long-term meditators. It suggests that meditation may help prevent age-related brain atrophy, a common condition in the elderly. A more recent study published in 2015 reinforced this finding. It showed less age-related brain atrophy in long-term meditators compared to those who don't meditate.[8]

Regular meditation is a form of self-directed neuroplasticity. You can use your mind to make positive long-lasting changes in the neuronal pathways of your brain. When you meditate on a regular basis, you get better at holding your attention in the present moment. This may translate into improved focus and less stress. You get better at processing sensory information. This may translate into you becoming more intuitive. You also become more self-aware. This may translate into better self-regulation of your autonomic nervous system. Regular meditation may even help prevent age-related brain atrophy, which has the potential to protect against memory loss and improve brain function as you age.

That's pretty epic! When we choose to rework our inner landscape and focus our attention on purpose, we break the bond of neurons habitually firing together and alter the plasticity of our brains. It also alters which neurotransmitters are released and forges new neural pathways.

Actively rewiring our brains for more efficient processing requires us to first acknowledge this as a possibility. Breaking old habits can feel daunting, but just knowing that our little daily actions amount to great changes in our physiology and psychology can make all the difference.

Taking personal responsibility in the maju way is about owning how much power you actually have over the quality of your responses, relationships, stories, and health. This principle is about cultivating self-awareness of your autopilot reactions without judgment and choosing moment to moment to feel your feelings and own them rather than project them.

Taking responsibility for your life is often associated with activities like properly managing your finances, honoring your commitments, and pulling your weight around the house and on the job. While these are very important, so is the quality of your experiences and inner life. The latter is rarely a topic of discussion in mainstream Western society or the public health and education system, yet it's critical to our success as humans.

What if you learned at an early age that your inner world determined the quality of your experiences and could be a catalyst for gene expression in your body? Would you be more mindful of ensuring you're taking daily steps to clear the noise from your mind? Would you make an effort to stay in the present moment to avoid autopilot syndrome? Would you be more inclined to use visualization techniques to change the pictures in your mind? Would you teach your children these principles in a comprehensible manner so they fully understand how their minds impact their overall physical health and quality of life? I'm fairly certain that if we all understood just how connected our minds and bodies are we would be more adamant about making those changes we've been putting off.

Whether we like it or not, the majority of our life is likely controlled by habitual responses with minimal conscious awareness. Many of these response patterns are extremely adaptive, like walking, eating and driving. They require little conscious attention because the process is committed to memory. That's great! However, in the same way we learned how to feed ourselves, we also learned how to respond emotionally to stressful situations, how to communicate our feelings to others, and how to behave appropriately in social situations.

Consider this: When someone upsets you, do you think about it, or does it just happen? When you get triggered, your mental, emotional, and behavioral response is likely an automatic reaction and not a conscious choice. The reality is that life does not happen to us, it just happens and we respond. The quality of our response is ultimately up to us.

By nature, we are creatures of habit who develop adaptive responses to survive. This highly successful survival function allows us to convert our experiences of the world into perceptions that determine the best way to respond to different situations. These response patterns are committed to our memory bank for easy retrieval, and we rely on them to get us through life. When we encounter a situation that resembles something we've experienced before, our autopilot system retrieves the file and presses play (oversimplified metaphor, of course). Sometimes the response encoded on the tape seems perfect for the situation, and other times it causes more harm than good.

However, it's important to know that the only thing that actually exists is the here and now. That means no tape from a past experience is ever going to be the perfect response to the present moment because each new moment is a unique moment.

These learned responses begin to develop during childhood as we observe the behavior of others and through our own trial and error. If we learned to view a situation as a threat, we will create a memory to avoid similar situations in the future. If we are unable to avoid repetitive exposure to the threat (i.e. physical or emotional abuse as a child) we will in turn develop adaptive coping mechanisms that helps us best survive the situation. Unfortunately, sometimes these learned responses can lead to fear of expressing our feelings, shame, emotional repression, or even disruptive outbursts when threatened. These repetitive reactions become habit, influencing our responses and how we handle stressful situations mentally, emotionally, and physically. These patterns make up our personality profile and influence all areas of our lives. But is that who we really are?

Living on autopilot means responding without self-awareness and falling victim to the logic of our own mind. Mindfulness-based practices help us regain control over our autopilot function by literally retraining our brain to become fully present in the moment, making us more aware of our automatic reaction. This pause gives us the ability to make a conscious choice to stop the response and just observe.

In general, our autopilot system is not a bad mechanism. It's necessary for survival and basic functioning. The issue arises when we self-identify with this system as the only mode to relate to the world, especially human interactions.

This is where personal responsibility over the quality of your inner world comes into play. Are you taking the necessary steps to ensure you are responding from the present moment? Are you actively training your brain to know how to pause? Does your mind race out of control with worrying thoughts but you choose to do nothing about it? Can you express yourself freely, or do you feel restrained in self-expression because of the stories you tell yourself? Are you spending all of your energy rehashing past stories and projecting onto others?

Where you choose to place your attention determines the quality of your experience. If you have an unsettling feeling and choose to make a story about why that is bad, you will feel bad. If you have an unsettling feeling and you're simply curious without judgment, allowing the feeling to be OK, and focus your attention on loving the part of yourself in pain, you will feel love. It's simply a shift in perception.

I can't even begin to describe the countless times my autopilot system failed me, especially in relationship with others. I would allow my rambling mind to focus on itself, planning what it might say next, yet failing to really hear the person in front of me. I would internalize criticism and use it as evidence to validate that I wasn't good enough.

I wasn't doing any of this intentionally; it was an automatic response from a part of myself that didn't feel good enough. It was only when I learned to pause and be present that I was able to make a conscious choice to respond differently.

SELF-SABOTAGE

We are all masters of sabotage from time to time. Our core beliefs and old habits are so engrained in our psychology and physiology that we unconsciously create issues to validate the need to hold onto our current perception. We are more committed to maintaining the status quo than having a new experience, even if the status quo means hateful self-talk and relationship drama. We have become biologically addicted to our current way of being and need to keep creating drama to get the same rush of chemicals to feel "normal."

If you've bought into the perception that you are not worthy, good enough, or loveable you will build a barrier to anything that challenges that core belief. Experiences will be filtered through this lens, keeping you in a vicious cycle of only seeing yourself and the world in one way.

It's fascinating to ponder the reality that our perceptions might be the only thing limiting us from blossoming into our full potential. Perceptions come in many shades, like tinted glasses that trick our minds into believing the world is a certain color. For me, fear-based perceptions shade my reality with a sense of darkness, resembling the shadows that linger in my unconscious. If I am committed to my attachment that the world is dark, then darkness is all I will see. Holding onto fear not only alters our perception of reality, it also draws a line in the sand for what we are capable of achieving.

Try opening yourself up to receive love. Accept the compliment instead of deflecting it. Raise your hand to ask the question even if your mind is telling you that you're stupid. Have a new experience that challenges your current way of being and watch how you grow. We are all a work in progress and stretching ourselves can sometimes be clumsy, like a child learning to walk. We don't judge a child for falling or wobbling when he's taking his first steps, so why would you judge yourself or anyone else? Baby steps add up and will eventually become enough evidence that change is possible.

BE CURIOUS RATHER THAN JUDGMENTAL

Owning our projections and checking our assumptions are critical components of personal responsibility in cultivating a Maju Mindset. That's because they define the quality of our inner world and outer experiences. It's easy to project future situations that haven't occurred yet, assuming they will resemble the past. Once you conclude that a particular outcome is imminent, you have immediately cut yourself off from having a different experience. The same is true for relationships. As soon as you assume how someone will respond, you've created a mental box around how you are willing to see them. Your past experiences with a person can be a great indicator for how you are willing to be around them. But just as you can shift your responses and view of reality, so can everyone else when they are ready. Let that be a possibility. And remember, our diversity is what makes this creative canvas of life a true masterpiece. Engage in dialogue that invites curiosity and watch the depth of your connection increase.

Ask yourself: If I'm feeling angry toward someone can I own that the emotion stems from something within myself? Am I willing to say, "I notice I am angry" versus "You made me angry?" If I'm frustrated, irritated, or feeling impatient due to a particular circumstance can I refrain from projecting those emotions outward and allow the process within myself to be OK?

Emotions are not bad. They are indicators of a deeper process unfolding within. It has little to do with the subject that made you fly over your edge, and more to do with what was triggered within you. Choosing to turn the mirror toward yourself when an unsettling emotion arises helps to shine a light on what's keeping you in that state of being. It's not necessary to understand the "why," as the mind will make every attempt to justify the logic and project outward once more, keeping you spinning in a circle. Instead, simply acknowledge the energy (or emotion) moving through your body without judgment. Once you are willing to take ownership of it, the light will illuminate the shadows of your mind and provide clarity on how to proceed. As you stay present to your inner experience, you will have more control over how to respond consciously.

Each person's path to liberation is unique and it does no good to compare ourselves to others. The life hurdles you have at the present moment are for you to overcome. For some, breaking an attachment to material possessions and habitual over-spending cultivates a sense of freedom. For others, stepping out of a scarcity mindset filled with lack and limitation helps them see how abundant their lives truly are. Everyone has a different story, set of experiences, and truths about how the world works. Be curious, not judgmental, and you will learn more than what your assumptions can tell you.

Cultivating genuine curiosity in conversation is an extremely important social trait as it helps override the automatic projections that generate unfounded assumptions. Curiosity also helps to keep you connected in the present moment with the other person. Get curious about what it might be like to be the other person and let go of your need to try to figure them out. There is no way you will ever fully know what it's like to be the other person. Check your assumptions when they come up. Maybe they are right, but maybe they aren't.

Now I am curious. What do you want for your life? What virtues do you strive for? Are you continually tested on your level of patience, acceptance, compassion, courage, accountability, trust, or humility? What are your relationships like? Who are you?

Approaching life with curiosity is also greatly helpful when challenging circumstances arise. You might ask yourself, what is it within me that is having such a hard time right now? Why do I keep seeing the same damn issue come up in my life, and what role might I be playing in creating it?

Continuing to not take responsibility for the life you are creating is a sure fire way to drive yourself insane. Trust me, I know. My man-made prison was filled with convincing stories that shaded my perception about my role in creating my reality.

"It's not my fault."

"He did this to me."

"How could they make me feel this way?"

"I have no power in this situation."

"I am the victim."

These stories keep us in state of victim consciousness and in a perpetual cycle of creating a crappy life. We're always trying to fix something "out there" and spend very little time addressing the root cause inside ourselves.

No matter what, you are not defined by your current circumstance nor are you stuck in one way of being in the world. The actions you choose to take in life may be the result of your internal motives, stressors, and habits, but you are not limited by them. Beyond the walls of your mind lies your true potential waiting for you to believe in what else might be possible.

DON'T BE AFRAID TO PLAY (HARD)

Approaching life through a lens of amusement has been life altering. When I am conscious that the negative tape in my mind is a pre-recorded message, I find myself amused at how it got there. When I see others expressing themselves in ways I disagree with, I am amused by my quick judgment. Amusement is a blend of playfulness and curiosity. It invites a mindset of objectivity and eases my emotional attachment to a situation.

If life feels too serious, that's an indicator that the pictures in my mind stem from a belief that life is hard and I am limited. It's at this moment that I make a conscious choice to shift my energy from limitations to possibilities.

Tapping my sense of amusement starts when I pretend I can alter the picture in my mind (because I actually can!) I often visualize that something off the wall and hilarious is happening. Immediately I notice a shift in my energy as if I pushed the button and a different view appeared. See, your Maju glasses are programmable. They are external reminders to check your bullshit at the door and do something different. But what do you want them to do? I've programmed mine to immediately prompt me to check my level of amusement. They send me back to a child's mind, where I become the superhero and anything is possible because I say so. From this perspective, everything changes. My mood improves. I don't feel the heaviness of seeing the situation as a burden, and I find it easier to let things go. That's pretty awesome if you ask me.

Look, tackling deep shit can feel like jumping into quicksand. It's dense, tiring, and sometimes feels like more of a burden than it's worth. Inviting a sense of childlike playfulness into your awareness is a great way to tap your imagination during difficult times. That's because it changes your relationship to the picture in your mind. Maybe under the quicksand is a hidden world, where all the treasure has been hidden away for only you to find. Think about how a child would tackle this opportunity. They would put on their goggles and flippers, dive in, go exploring, and they wouldn't come up empty handed. And it wouldn't be quicksand anymore, it would be a hole filled with candy corn. And Jello! (you can turn it into wine if that soothes your little adult soul.)

Every picture in your mind is energy that triggers a physiological response producing feelings such as avoidance, resistance, and fear. Fortunately, the pictures can be transmuted simply by placing your attention on them and calling bullshit. But first, this takes awareness that there is another possible perspective and shifting your lens to what you really want to believe.

The emotional conviction to do something different paints a clear picture of possibility that triggers a physiological response. This allows you to align with what you truly want and transmutes the old imagery. I have watched thousands of coaching clients create instantaneous changes simply by playing with their imagination. The children were right all along.

Can you imagine if your life was guided by the innate curiosity of your inner child and the awareness and wisdom of your adult self? I'm fairly certain some of our inner children would require everyone to wear tutu's on Tuesdays and make adults use training wheels in life. I can hear my inner child saying, "How on earth do the adults keep bumping into that same wall? Don't they see it? No, of course not. They're not looking in the right direction. They have forgotten they have a world inside themselves. If only they could forget everything someone else told them and remember who they were originally, maybe that would fix things. Maybe they should just close their eyes and let their inner child paint a new picture of possibility. These adults are in trouble I tell you. Someone needs to play with them." If we are willing to play with our inner children they will play with us in life. I can't imagine anything more fulfilling.

It's only a matter of time before each one of us throws in the towel of mediocrity to live freely once more. We know far too much about the mind-body connection and the detrimental effects of suppressive and unconscious conditioning to continue playing that old game. We are an evolving species equipped with life-changing resources at our finger tips and we must choose to expand ourselves into the best we can be. No other time in history have we been so cross pollenated with ideas and wisdom from around the world. We need to find the courage to rise up and make a conscious choice to take personal responsibility for the quality of our lives in order to flourish. Evolution begins you!

THE GLASSES OF AMY

Meet Amy Silverman. I met her while traveling in Holland. I attended a class she taught called Connection Play Shop and was struck by her presence and playful perspective on exploring the depths of our inner world. This is her perspective on personal responsibility.

Tell us a little about yourself.

I am committed to bringing people together through play, connection, collaboration, self-expression, and creativity. My passion for igniting human connection led me to build The Connection Movement, a rapidly growing international community that dives into self-discovery, transformation, and deep, earnest communication through events, workshops, coaching programs, social experiments, and retreats.

I am a passionate connector with a natural instinct toward big vision and action. Through The Connection Movement, I launched circling and authentic relating communities in New York City, Johannesburg, Cape Town, South Florida, and South Carolina, with more cities to follow soon. I am devoted to coaching leaders and facilitators who aspire to build tribes and run thriving local communities and businesses.

What does personal responsibility mean to you?

I like to think of responsibility as the ability to respond with choice and intention, which ultimately means knowing oneself, challenging oneself to define and distinguish our inner workings and how we relate to different emotional triggers, stimulus, people, and scenarios. It also means being proactive and knowing our needs and how to meet them, either by ourselves or by engaging support from others.

What does projection mean to you?

Projection means many things: Simply defined, we look at others and assume that they are like us, or are like our idea of them. In doing so, we allow ourselves to ignore or miss what is actually present and diminish authentic intimacy and connection with each other. There's a tendency in humans to focus on behaviors in others that we deny, or are unaware of, in ourselves.

What does taking ownership over our feelings mean and how do you see this impacting relationships?

Taking ownership of our feelings means recognizing what is mine and what is yours. It's knowing why you're feeling the way you are and identifying the source of those feelings as your own. It's about communicating in a way that doesn't presume that your perception of things is what's true or what's true for the other person. In relationships, this has a huge impact as it leaves space for communication and contact without blame, presumption, or projection.

How does the concept of play help with a person's sense of wellbeing?

In my view, play is the way humans learn and grow - we experiment, explore, fail, try again, and create. An attitude of play sets the tone for life being an exploration and always unfolding, which minimizes stress and boosts one's sense of wellbeing. It allows us to soften our grip on outcomes, relax our minds, and reach for opportunities that we might not otherwise allow ourselves to experience.

FINE TUNING YOUR GLASSES

It's your turn! The following exercise is designed to help you take steps right now to sharpen your level of self-awareness. Programming your new Maju Glasses to include personal responsibility as an important and epic perspective requires you to do the work (or as I prefer to call it, playtime – it's all perspective!)

Play Date #1 – Who Are You?

House rules: Answer the questions honestly and go with your first instinct. The answers will likely morph over time, but let's assess what comes up first and then you can decide later if that's what you actually want to perceive. Observe any self-talk that arises with as much curiosity as possible. Points will be deducted if you try to be perfect and over analyze. You only get two slipups and then I win. Go!

I am _____

My intention is _____

My greatest desire is _____

When I feel angry, I _____

When I'm scared, I _____

I expect people to _____

I judge people when _____

When I feel uncomfortable feelings I (choose one)

_____ Share my feelings with others

_____ Process my feelings alone

_____ Push it down and don't address it again

_____ Other: _____

My level of personal responsibility (aka, I own my shit) is (circle one)

Epic!   Kind of awesome   Not that cool   Damn it!

➢ Please elaborate: _____

_____

_____

How much do you agree: I am open to the idea of meditation to cultivate self-awareness and reprogram my brain (circle one)

Definitely!   I'd consider it   Hmm…   You're crazy

➢ Please elaborate: _____

_____

_____

I am in tune with my feelings (circle one)

Oh yeah!   For the most part   I tried to avoid them   Feelings?

➢ Please elaborate: _____

_____

_____

I own my projections and judgments (circle one)

As much as I can   Pretty often   Kinda-sorta-maybe-no   Nah

➢ Please elaborate: _____

_____

_____

I believe I am truly limitless (circle one)

Hell yeah!   On good days   Not sure yet   Nope

➢ Please elaborate: _____

_____

_____

If I continue down the same path, my life will _____

_____

_____

_____

_____

If I dream into possibilities of what could be, my life will _____

_____

_____

_____

_____

Name six positive feelings you'd like to experience regularly
(For example, confident, secure, happy, vibrant, joyful, alive, peaceful, calm, abundant, focused, loved, worthy, free, etc):

1. _____   4. _____

2. _____   5. _____

3. _____   6. _____

➤ Now take a moment and allow yourself to feel the above feelings as if they were true right now. Don't hold back – this is the moment of seeding a new possibility, plus it floods your body with new chemical messengers. You lose points if you skip it, FYI. Notice if you hear any part of yourself that opposes receiving the positive feelings. Just be the observer and continue to be present to the seeds you are sowing.

YOUR MISSION

That sounds way better than homework. Plus it's just a play date and I think that would be illegal.

➤ For the next seven days, I want you to repeat the feeling exercise above, using the same words you selected. The longer you inoculate your body with the new feelings, the more you will shift your energy. Notice if any images of possibility come to mind. Perhaps you can visualize what life would be like if you often felt this way. Own it because it's yours to have. If you notice any mental pictures of lack or limitation, see if you can blow them up and make them go POOF. Keep a journal of anything that arises. If you notice yourself avoiding this exercise, just know my inner child will find you and call bullshit on your resistance. She's nice, but feisty when she doesn't get her way. Let's not go down that path.

The Hearts Call
by Kristi Lee Schatz

Reality is the totality of what we've been told
Biased to see things before they unfold.
Assuming we know and assigning roles
Is the epitome of missing the essence of the soul.

Yet if we knew the world wasn't what we thought
We wouldn't spend so much time defining our plot.
Those stories that loop and keep us confined
Are the blinding beliefs that control our mind.

The perceptions of doubt and fear of the unknown
Limit our ability to see what wants be shown.
The light, the truth, the possibilities beyond
What our minds could fathom if we were to actually respond
To the crazy, absurd, and unimaginable ideas
That drift through our awareness and give us the chills.

It's those moments of knowing what our heart desires
That enlivens our soul and deeply inspires.
The action to move, to shift, and to change
A life out of balance is worth the exchange.
Of time, of tears, of the monumental growth
That will clear the way for a new conscious oath.

A recommitment to Self and the potential within
Letting go of our definition from way back when.
A vow to nurture the authentic being
That can build a life from truly seeing.
The beauty, the mystery, the wonderment of all
and sit in stillness to hear the hearts true call.

Maju Style

Do you put on a mask to impress others, prove your worth, or hide your vulnerability? If you answered yes, could you please do me a favor and knock it off? I want to see all of you.

> It's Time To Get Real!

5

PRINCIPLE 2: AUTHENTICITY

Authenticity is about being honest and true to yourself. When you hide behind a façade because you think that is what the other person wants to see, you lose sight of what your unique self can bring to the relationship.

A study published in the Journal of Counseling Psychology explored the notion that living authentically is a fundamental component of a healthy life.[9] In the article, the authors state:

"In many mainstream counseling psychology perspectives, authenticity is seen as the most fundamental aspect of well-being.[10,11,12,13,14] These researchers see authenticity not simply as an aspect or precursor to well-being but rather the very essence of well-being and healthy functioning... Authentic living involves behaving and expressing emotions in such a way that is consistent with the conscious awareness of physiological states, emotions, beliefs, and cognitions. In other words, authentic living involves being true to oneself in most situations and living in accordance with one's values and beliefs... Authenticity involves the extent to which one accepts the influence of other people and the belief that one has to conform to the expectations of others. Humans are fundamentally social beings, and both self-alienation and authentic living are affected by the social environment.[15]"

It's pretty difficult to just be yourself in society when you don't fully accept yourself as you are. It's even more challenging if you fear your authentic expression would socially isolate you. We all want to feel like we belong. This is a universal shared experience that dates back to the evolutionary benefit of sticking with the herd for survival and reproducing offspring.[16] However, there is also an innate desire for "being yourself" which can compete with your desire to belong.[17]

But do we really want to belong if the acceptable societal norm means sacrificing our freedom of authentic expression? Does anyone really desire to repress their true feelings? Of course not, yet we do it anyways. Fear of being judged, rejected, not good enough, or any other label we're trying to avoid, keeps us in the habit of hiding ourselves. So how do we overcome the competing forces from within and without? How do we honor our authentic self and our desire to belong?

The second principle of the Maju Mindset is about seeing the world through a lens that allows for both of these to be a possibility. When I understand my deep truth and I am willing to take ownership of my feelings, I am more likely to feel secure with who I am. When I understand we all have the innate desire to be unique and belong, my resistance to showing up authentically lessens. I'm OK with the fact the other person may disagree, or even judge me. We are all different. The social pressure I feel to hold back from expressing my authentic self stems from a fear of not being accepted as I am. When I begin to cultivate self-acceptance knowing I'm a glorious mess in process just like everyone else, I tend to reveal more of my truth to others. I also notice that my authentic sharing tends to deepen my connection to the other person in more cases than not.

When I combine the first and second principle of the Maju Mindset, here is what I begin to perceive about the world:

I am aware that I am the creator of my experience and responsible for my feelings. I speak from a space of personal ownership and do not play victim. I recognize everyone is different and I choose to be curious rather than judgmental. I understand everyone has a desire to belong while honoring their uniqueness. I see the current social climate as sometimes stifling to our individual expression and I choose to break this cycle by honoring my truth and being present to other people's experience. I recognize honest communication that isn't filled with projection is the best way to be heard. When I feel like I need to hide my true self I commit to stepping back and looking within to understand the part of me that is scared of full expression. I know the more I show up authentically the more liberated and connected I will feel. Integrating these two principles for myself will help me to model to the next generation a more fulfilling way to live.

This perspective continues to transform my relationships and outlook on life. While I gravitate toward individuals and groups who share the value of authentic connection, I will admit I am still challenged in certain social circumstances to just be myself. This usually occurs when I'm intimated. I use those moments as an opportunity to observe the part of myself that feels the need to hold back. As I become more self-aware and self-accepting, the less likely I am to use a social mask as a coping mechanism to meet my need of belongingness.

For much of my life I didn't feel seen. Partly because I was hiding certain aspects of myself, and partly because I felt projected onto. It took me years to learn that my perceived imperfections are actually perfect. I don't need to be someone different at work than I am at home. I don't have to look like everyone else to feel like I belong. I don't have to hide how I felt in connection to others, whether it was positive or negative, so long as I am willing to take ownership of my feelings. I commit to staying in connection with the other person through curiosity, even when tension arises. My entire life has changed through this perceptual and behavior shift.

THE MANY PARTS OF YOU

You, my friend. are multifaceted! Understanding that you are not your thoughts, beliefs, defense mechanisms, past experiences, or societal roles can greatly help in overcoming your habitual way of being. What if you have a new experience that challenges your existing identity and makes you change your mind or the role you play in the world? Then who are you?

My depression was prompted by an identity crisis because I was so attached to who I thought I was and the role I played in the world. To change meant a death of my old self and a birth of a new self. But even that self was temporary. So if I'm not my thoughts, experiences, roles, or personality, who am I? And who is the one questioning? In my belief system, the true self is the Spirit – the observer behind the scenes. It's an unbound and pure state of consciousness that is not self-identified with any particular part of my personality self.

However, 1 am still human and I have many facets of my personality self that influence my daily choices, perceptions, and level of authentic expression. These are the parts that play on autopilot and remain largely outside of my conscious awareness. Some parts are extremely adaptive while others wreck havoc in my life.

Think about this way: when you feel hurt it's helpful to take a step back and notice the part of you that is upset, angry, or in pain. Remember you are not your stories or perceptions; you have them and you can shift them when you become conscious of their presence. The parts of you that are wounded from past experiences have created their own coping strategies to handle certain situations and impact your relationships and habits. Along the journey, you begin to identify with these parts as who you are. In transpersonal psychology, a field of psychology that explores the transcendent and spiritual dimensions of human development, these parts are called subpersonalities.

The following excerpt provided by Natasha Dern is from her article, "Subpersonalities: Who's Calling The Shots?"[18] It offers a perspective on how these parts of ourselves influence our lives:

> When you over identify with a particular wound it creates an emotional blueprint within your emotional body referred to as a subpersonality. Without realizing, you begin to build your whole identity and life around this blueprint, thus believing it is who you really are. Your subpersonality is not the real YOU, it is a part of you but it is not you. To make this distinction is crucial. You need to realize that a subpersonality suffering from lack of self-esteem or low self-worth is only a part of you, an extension of your emotional body. Rather than identifying yourself as 'I am insecure,' restate it as 'a part of me is insecure.' This kind of discernment is truly empowering. It removes this insecure subpersonality from the position of power and puts you in the driver's seat."

Subpersonalities, in transpersonal psychology, are personas or pieces of the personality, such as beliefs, thoughts, feelings, intentions, and agendas, that have a life of their own.

There's the rebel and the martyr, the seducer and the saboteur, the judge and the critic and a host of others, each with their own mythology, all co-existing within a person. Issues and conflict arise when the polarity of a subpersonality becomes imbalanced. When opposing tensions sets in, the mind is clouded with conflicting views, which hinders its ability to make decisions that are appropriate. How can you figure out which subpersonalities are calling the shots?

Start by taking stock of your outlook on life, reviewing your behavior in various situations, and all the ways you can express yourself in any given moment. When you recognize a subpersonality you will be able to step outside it and observe its complex nature. By doing this, you will no longer completely identify with that subpersonality. Instead, you will begin to see the many faces of your soul and appreciate the value of each one.

We have many subpersonalities within us, each one of them has a story to tell. Each one views the world differently. Each one interprets the events of life differently. You need to acquaint yourself with those that are controlling your behavior, your thinking or your choices. Some subpersonalities are not harmful; they exist to support your well-being. Focus on the ones that constantly provoke, invoke, react or attack. These subpersonalities are hurt and angry, wounded and in need of healing. To work with these energies requires patience and a certain level of detachment in order to relate to them objectively. As mentioned above, the way you start is by identifying which subpersonality you have given power to, which one you have enabled to rule your life. You need to shift your thinking and begin to perceive these subpersonalities as parts of you rather than them being you.

Learning to objectively identify my subpersonalities was a critical step in my personal evolution towards authentic self-expression. This process allowed me to step out of my habitual way of relating to the world and see the bigger picture of my full being. My life use to be ruled by the perceptions of my inner critic. It was the dominant part of my autopilot personality profile that filtered what I could and shouldn't express. When triggered, it would switch the pictures in my mind to view the world in a particular way. When I became more self-aware, I realized the inner critic was hindering my authentic self-expression and was no longer serving my highest good. In the next chapter I will share how I overcame the stronghold of this part using the power of vulnerability (the inner critics worst enemy.)

"All sub-personalities contain a version of the true self. They amplify some vital aspect to suit a situation, but cut us off from other parts of the self in the process.[19]"
- Richard Boileau

SHAKE IT UP!

Do you openly and honestly share your feelings with others from a space of personal ownership? Do you hide parts of yourself that you are ashamed of? What if you could deepen your connection and intimacy with others by revealing more of who you are?

Many of us find it challenging to share our full self because of the social agreements and roles we play in our relationships. The hidden contracts between two people often govern the appropriate type of communication that is allowed to occur. Breaking this social contract often results in temporary tension.

System dynamics has shown that introducing new information into a system will often produce a little chaos as the unit as a whole attempts to return to homeostasis, or balance. We see this dynamic play out in systems across the board, including ecosystems, political systems, social systems, and family systems. The beautiful thing about personal growth work is that you don't have to change anyone but yourself to shift the whole system. And it's not your responsibility to change anyone else. When you show up differently the system around you will shift automatically to adapt. Many of us live in fear of this reality and therefore avoid it at all costs.

During graduate school, we were given an assignment to challenge the habitual system dynamics that existed within our family. As we approached Thanksgiving break, we were instructed to go home and sit in a different seat at the dinner table and simply observe the reaction of the system. It seemed silly at the time, but it actually produced some real tension with some of the students. Many people felt that there was no way they could go home and try to take their father's seat at the head of the table. The system just wouldn't allow for it. I completely understood. I would never want to go home to my family and take my one of my parents' seats at the table. It would feel like a rude thing to do. But the point was to show how certain behaviors become the status quo, no matter how silly they may seem. Challenging the dynamics of a system may result in tension and most of us try to avoid that at all cost, even if we're not fully content with the setup. Becoming aware of the roles you ascribe to and the roles you assign others will help shine light on the dynamics at play in your life.

I am constantly observing my surroundings, watching how other people behave in social settings and how I play into the dynamic of suppressing myself. I have come a long way in terms of self-acceptance and relating authentically. But I have yet to experience all that life has to offer and I'm continuously challenged with new circumstances that provide deeper insight to the hidden layers of my being. The more grounded I become in self-love and compassion, the less I am influenced by the opinions and projections of others.

If we were all consciously taking responsibility for our thoughts, feelings, and behaviors we would likely see a rise in compassion and forgiveness. We would be more inclined to connect heart-to-heart. But first, it begins with each one of us making that choice.

OPTICAL ILLUSION

Let's talk about the destructive art of placing people on a pedestal as it relates to authenticity. We've all admired someone for their courage, wisdom, or success. Teachers, speakers, celebrities, and other successful people are usually placed higher on the social ladder for their superhuman skills. The Oprah's and Richard Branson's of the world don't seem like the rest of us. But what if they are? What if they were raised with the same societal expectations and fears of the unknown? What if one day they woke up and realized they were the only ones limiting their potential? The only difference between them and the rest of us is they had the courage and trust to take the leap and honor their intuition that they were capable of manifesting a new reality.

It's easy to make assumptions about what another person's journey to success must have been like. It's even easier to compare yourself to them, resting in the belief that they are somehow different. But placing them on a pedestal keeps you feeling small, inferior, and powerless. These projections can be quite debilitating if they are internalized and used to measure your self-worth. We aspire to be like them, yet minimize our actual ability to do so. We have mastered the unconscious art of pedestal building.

When you build a pedestal for others you disconnect from seeing their true self. You objectify them, turning them into a tool for your projections. Your desires and insecurities become the lens through which you see them. But that's not who they truly are.

I want to make it clear that admiring someone for their brilliance isn't a bad thing. It's great to recognize the accomplishments of someone who is living out their passion and to aspire to do the same. These are our models of what's possible. It only becomes a problem when we project onto them that they are different than us and that we can't have the same reality because we aren't good enough, rich enough, smart enough, or worth it. That illusion keeps us in a vicious cycle of creating the same damn limitations.

Let's not forget about the other side of this coin. The act of ditch digging occurs when you assume you are better than someone else. You're not necessarily attempting to build a pedestal for yourself, but rather a ditch for them. Ditches are communicated through subtle aggressions in verbal communication and body language. Your thoughts are laced with judgments of superiority. As soon as you dig a ditch for someone to lie in, you've made it difficult to fully connect with them.

It's hard to see eye-to-eye when someone is above or below you.

While I didn't fancy ditch digging, I was a master of pedestal building. Anyone who held a higher degree or status in the community was better than me. I paraded around in my mask hoping they wouldn't detect that I was less than them. It's hard to know yourself when all you can hear are the tapes that tell you should be more like them. I suffered from a debilitating core belief that I wasn't good enough, which eventually turned into a severe case of social anxiety, especially when I was around someone I placed on a pedestal.

Vulnerably sharing your true self while standing eye-to-eye and heart-to-heart with a stranger is liberating beyond your wildest dreams. What if you could let others authentically see you for who you truly are without censorship? What if you could lead conversations with your "first truth first," letting the other person know what's truly alive for you in that present moment? Knowing that all of our lights have been dimmed through the human condition greatly helps in breaking down the barriers toward deep, meaningful connection. When you are a mirror for another person's magnificence, it ultimately reflects back your own brilliance.

Here's a metaphor to chew on: Have you ever witnessed an adult dancing on the sidewalk as if no one was watching? This act is likely to stun most bystanders and trigger judgments about their ridiculous behavior. It could also produce envy for their sense of freedom, fearlessness, and exuberant self-acceptance. We can't control what other people think of us, but we can free ourselves from the burden of having to care.

"And those who were seen dancing were thought to be insane by those who could not hear the music."
- **Friedrich Wilhelm Nietzsche**

-

The person dancing at the bus stop to the song blaring through their headphones may be an easy target for judgment, but could you do this? How would your inner critic feel if someone judged you? Would you be consumed with thoughts of impressing onlookers? Perhaps dancing on the sidewalk is a form of movement meditation that could liberate you from your inhibitions and fears. What if you could let go of all thoughts and reach a state of contentment, joy, and unwavering self-love? What if your authentic self wanted to let loose and groove with the tunes, would you do it?

This metaphor easily lends itself to all areas of your life, like how you hold yourself back from freely expressing your authentic self in public, how you conform to other people's expectations to please or impress them, and how you criticize yourself and others for not following your man-made rulebook. Call it human nature or learned behavior. Either way, it impacts your health, happiness and relationships.

As we progress forward embracing creativity, holistic wellness, and community collaboration, it is essential that we examine the social norms that discourage us from fully showing up in the world. Each person plays an important role in this collective dance and deserves the opportunity to freely express themselves without the weight of fear, judgment, or shame.

Imagine living in a community where you feel safe to let go of your need to impress or judge others because deep down inside you know that you are good enough and so is everyone else. If we gave ourselves permission to dance ecstatically in the streets we may just see a revolution of self-love permeate our cities. This would be true freedom.

The next time you witness a dancing rebel on the sidewalk, observe yourself. Perhaps it's time to lay down your judging sword, take off your protective armor and join them in the celebration of being human. It's up to each of us to choose how we want to create our communities, and it starts one person at a time. What will you choose?

THE GLASSES OF SARA

This is Sara Ness. She is a warrior in my book. Her experiential workshops, life perspective, playfulness, humility, and wisdom has helped shape who I am today. She is one of the brave souls breaking the mold for what is possible for authentic relating. This is her perspective on authenticity.

Tell us a little about yourself.

I felt like school taught me everything except what I was really interested in: how to interact with other human beings. I grew up lonely. My main contact with the world as a child was through books. Before I got to college, I'd been going to a tiny all-girls school for eight years.

Midway through college, I decided to take a year off and film a documentary on intentional living communities. These include co-ops, cohousing developments, and communes. They've become increasingly popular in the last few years as more social and often cheaper housing options. For me, living in a co-op was the first time I had to learn how to be around other people on a constant basis, and I was fascinated by the growth and dynamics that emerged from that pressure cooker. During that experience I encountered Authentic Relating. A man I met began talking to me with presence, curiosity, and honesty. I was in love.

When I got back from my trip, I began leading Authentic Relating Games in Houston, and I started a community in Austin. I was excited and terrified to take on leadership, but people liked it, and the Authentic Relating community gradually became my closest group of friends. I began holding retreats in conjunction with the Houston crew and training facilitators to help. A year later, when I graduated from college, two of my facilitators and I started a business.

What I love about my work is that it always keeps me on my edge. Every time I run a new training, or work with a new community, or form a new collaboration, I'm scared. Will I be of value? Will they trust me? Will I seem like a fraud? What keeps me going is that my work seems to provide value. I think it's one of the best ways I could spend my time. I'm learning, growing, and teaching every day, and I finally understand, for the most part, how to connect with others in a fulfilling way.

What does authenticity mean to you?

Honesty. Not just with ourselves and others, but with all the parts of ourselves and others. We have many facets of being, and authenticity means being willing to truthfully look at and strive to represent all of who we are.

What is authentic relating and how does it impact the quality of our relationships?

Authentic relating is a practice of identifying our thoughts, feelings, motivations, and perceptions, and communicating those to others in a way that can be heard. It makes relationship a place of growth and revelation. When I'm being honest and staying open to your truth, we have the chance to meet at a level where childhood trauma, value conflicts, and miscommunication can be heard, or even healed.

What struggles have you faced around being authentic?

Right now, my biggest struggles involve knowing what my truth is and communicating it when I'm frozen. I'm always discovering different levels of what I think, feel, or believe, and when I find a new facet of my being - usually through watching my response to some new life stress - I can feel inauthentic. 'Dammit! I've been saying I don't want to go out because I thought I had too much work, but really I was just avoiding anxiety. Some authenticity teacher I am.' That's frustrating and I try to practice gentleness toward myself when it happens. I also have moments when I feel frozen and can't speak, especially when I'm scared.

Why are you so passionate about helping others live authentic lives?

It tends to make us happier, more creative, and more engaged, since bringing half of ourselves to a situation naturally leads to everybody waiting on everybody else to have the good idea or say the hard thing. What I'm most interested in, though, is helping us to live related lives. We can be honest all day, but if it falls on deaf ears, we tend to end up unhappy. Understanding each other could save our relationships. If countries start doing it, and leaders start doing it, it might just save the world.

What advice would you give to someone who really wants to bring their full self to the world but might be a little scared?

Think about why you're doing it. What reason is strong enough to have you express yourself, even if some people don't like the change? When you begin shifting how you are, your life inevitably shifts with you. You may lose friends, change work, or even move. If you stay grounded in your intention - what one of my teachers calls your "why bother?" - you'll have a compass pointing home.

FINE TUNING YOUR GLASSES

Ah, another play date with my new buddy! OK, so today we're going to role play. I hope your imagination is sharp because I'm pretty good at this game.

Play Date #2 – Name That Part

The rules of engagement are simple: Identify a part of yourself by giving it a name (externalizing helps us to become a neutral observer, plus it's fun to act like we're in kindergarten). Some parts you love and other parts you wish could be thrown into a river with a heavy cement block and hidden from sight for ever and ever – until someone comes along and finds you out and then you're in big trouble because you have to lie your ass off to save face – don't do that. There are no losers in this game, but you must play or you will piss off my inner child, and no one wants to do that. She's small, but mighty (and I think she has a pet dragon, the last I checked.) Go!

Meet _____ (name it), this is the part of me that shows up when I feel _____. When they are activated in me, they usually acts like this: _____

_____

_____

_____

_____

This is what I think about this part: _____

_____

This is what I imagine my friends would think about this part:

_____

_____

If I could say anything to this part, I would say: _____

_____

_____

This is how they would reply to what I said: _____

_____

_____

What does this part of me need? _____

_____

YOUR MISSION

Continue a dialogue with this part of yourself and simply notice what arises. The more you understand how this part influences your life, the easier it will be to detect when it's triggered.

Stepping into the Light
By Kristi Lee Schatz

Brilliance is the illumination of light from within
Seeing yourself fully and acknowledging where you've been.
It's taking the time to release what's old
And stepping on the edge and learning to be bold.

It's to feel alive in the presence of Being
And to sit with what arises that is truly freeing.
Escaping, denying and numbing creates walls
That blocks your brilliance and perpetuates your falls.
It's those cracks in the surface from the knocks of life
That are exactly what you need to shatter your strife.

Restricted by fear and living unclear
Are simply signs of avoiding that dreadful tear.
Beneath the surface of your harden armor
Lies the brilliant whisper that will help you garner.
The truth and strength required to be free
Of the man-made prison that guards you from the ke.y

Your brilliance is waiting beyond the gate
Of your mind's control and persuasive debate.
Those perceptions that keep you stuck in your state
Will paralyze you from the courage to create.
Those buried emotions have a toxic effect
Creating habits to avoid, defend, and deflect.
Trust me I was numb feeling insignificant like a speck
And almost lost my life from a lack of self-respect.

Not trusting the whisper that screams with grace
Causes many to withdraw from their unstable base.

The world is yearning for you to reveal
The magnificence within that is completely still.
The stillness that is alive with a voice so real
It's hard to deny its lingering appeal.

But to trust something so elusive, intangible, and quite surreal
Is to surrender your mind's control over the wheel.

Trusting the voice is the reason we're here
To remember, experience, and let go of our fear.
For life is a series of valuable lessons
That can lift your spirits or damn you from depression.

It's up to you to choose the way
Just know that the sky is not always grey.
For the light from within will reveal your sense of play
Bringing hope and joy to a once gloomy day.

Shift your perception of the world you're creating
And life will hand you what you've been awaiting.
Communicate your truth, feel your worth
And understand you've been perfect since your birth.

Happiness may fade with the shades of the moon
Which are just cycles provided to help you cocoon.
Taking you away from all that is mundane
And releasing the old that caused so much pain.

It's to evolve and transform from all that was
And remember your brilliance simply because.
Without your engagement the world is at a loss
For each of us need to become our own boss.
To take control of our emotions and relations
Is to birth a new earth filled with conscious nations.

Still the chaos of your conditioned mind
And you too will see your worries are benign.
By taking the time to put yourself first
You model to the children how to quench their thirst.
Seeing their light as fuel from their soul
Will guide them to seeing themselves as whole.

Sit in awe, be curious, and alive
And you'll discover you too can actually thrive.

Maju Style

Becoming a vulnerable badass takes time. Eventually you'll discover the power of being naked and afraid. There's magic on the other side of your bubble. I promise. You got this!

> Vulnerable Badassery

6

PRINCIPLE 3: VULNERABILITY

Try these glasses on for size. Expressing yourself vulnerably with others can deepen your connection and add more depth to your relationship. Showing your real, raw, and vulnerable parts increases your self-confidence and can accelerate your growth and healing process. Suppressing parts of yourself that you are ashamed of creates walls in your mind and stress in your body. In the Maju Mindset, vulnerability is not a weakness; it's an act of courage that many shy away from. This perspective allows you to tackle your fears when they arise, which paves the path for self-realization and true freedom.

Vulnerability is a way to express the unspoken or unacknowledged. It's to externalize the inner world and make it tangible so you can see more clearly what is really at hand and how to move forward. In and of itself, this can be transformational.

Our fear of being emotionally vulnerable is the biggest hindrance to our personal growth and our collective evolution. Most of us are walking around armored and scared. We weren't taught about emotions. We learned socially acceptable ways to process (or not process) our feelings throughout the course of our lives. Many of us are capable of flipping a switch to numb ourselves when uncomfortable feelings arise. This can range from anger, sadness, fear, and even love. But what if we shifted the conversation at an earlier age to discuss emotions as a critical component of living a healthy life? What if the next generation was raised with the understanding that being vulnerable is an essential process of growth? Perhaps this shift in mindset could prevent stress-related diseases and mental disturbances for the future leaders of our world. Perhaps it would curb reactionary behavior and finally break the cycle of blame and shame.

The most badass people I have encountered are warriors in the field of vulnerability. They demonstrate permission to be themselves, responsibility for the quality of their inner world, and a commitment to deepening their intimacy with others. These people are my heroes. When I witness someone sharing their deeper truths, even if it's challenging for them to express, I often experience deep appreciation for their willingness to show themselves to me. I tend to see more of myself in them than I did before, thus deepening our connection. It also opens my heart because I realize they are being courageous and I wish the same for my life.

LEANING INTO THE EDGE

We all have skeletons in the closet, the messy, unprocessed stuff that we're ashamed of or don't fully want to acknowledge. We fear others will judge us for what we have hidden from sight or for the things we don't like about ourselves. We fear having to experience shame from being imperfect. We project the worst case scenario on the journey inward, creating an illusion of an uncomfortable experience that we would rather avoid.

I will be the first to admit, opening yourself up vulnerably and sharing your true feelings is uncomfortable. It can feel like leaning into the tip of a sharp knife on purpose. Extreme analogy, yes, but this is how intense our minds believe the process is going to be and why we make every attempt to avoid it.

We've all heard the saying, "That person really knows how to push my buttons." It's not them, it's you. It's the unprocessed stuff that you don't accept about yourself that creates the button in the first place. If you have yet to lean into your own edge, you sure as hell don't want someone else to lean into it. The longer you walk around with your triggered self on standby, the longer you will wait to live a truly happy and healthy life.

Jumping over our man-made line is scary because we don't know the impact it could have on our life. As humans, we place a high value on safety and clarity. Vulnerability challenges both of those. But is safety really that important? What if safety had less to do with what was happening out there and more to do with what's happening inside you? Sure, some situations pose a physical threat, but most just threaten our sense of self.

Despite being truly limitless, we tend to box ourselves into a comfort zone. Leaning into the edge makes us vulnerable simply because we have been attached to our so-called safe programming. This likely stems from a fear of the unknown. What will happen if I no longer see the world this way? If I admit this, will everything change?

Our current perception raises a red flag, signaling a physiological process to STOP, not because it's bad for us, but because we have convinced our body over a lifetime that what lies outside of our comfort zone should be avoided. It's simply a reaction and it's completely normal. Breaking the habit requires us to have a new experience, which will replace the old tape with a new framework of possibility.

VULNERABLE BADASSERY

Becoming a vulnerable badass isn't a onetime occurrence of being vulnerable. It's a way of life. I spent the first part of my life repressing my feelings, which not only numbed me to pain, but also to joy. I held grudges toward others, reacted passive aggressively, and never thought I was capable of reaching my potential. Now, I fully experience my feelings and take ownership of them to the best of my ability, no matter how uncomfortable it feels. By doing this, I stay in the present moment and don't hold onto the energy.

Learning to stretch outside of my comfort zone was the result of a monumental leap I let my heart make. Graduate school was calling out to me. But not just any school. It had to be Transpersonal Psychology. I didn't know why at the time, but an overwhelming churning sensation in my heart flared up every time I thought about it, guiding me strongly to this educational path. My ego found satisfaction that I would earn a master's degree from my training, but my heart knew it wasn't about the credential. I had to be vulnerable and jump off the metaphorical cliff and take the deep dive into myself. It was time, and this was the vehicle that would guide me. A few months prior to graduate school, I tied the knot with a sweet man who agreed to leap with me. We left our comfortable nest in the redwood forest, just south of the Oregon border, and moved to San Francisco. Neither one of us were quite prepared for what would unfold over the next two years.

As you'll soon discover, this wasn't your typical psychology graduate school. Of course we took the standard classes required for licensure like psychopharmacology, research methods, group theory, and multicultural counseling. But this school had a unique quirk. We didn't just intellectually learn how the mind processes information, we dove in experientially through meditation, somatic work, aikido, group process, spiritual studies, human sexuality courses, and creative expression modalities like art, poetry, movement, and psychodrama. The further we journeyed into ourselves, the easier it became to sit with a client without our own stuff getting triggered. I have no doubt that this experience was the tipping point that catapulted me into a life of vulnerable self-exploration and expression. It laid a solid foundation upon which I have built my life. But it wasn't easy. The time had come to finally take the power back from my inner critic and it required a high level of courage to step out of my own damn way and do something different.

POETRY THERAPY, OH CRAP!

I dreaded my first class. Not because I didn't find value in the content, but because I knew the experience would push me outside of my comfort zone. Experiential learning was the name of the game and I was ill equipped for what was to come.

When you feel emotionally suppressed and lack the necessary confidence and courage to speak your truth, a poetry therapy class is going to scare the crap out of you. Not because writing is hard, but because your turn to share in front of the group will arise, revealing your nervous voice, shaky hands, and overwhelming self-doubt.

I sat silently class after class, taking good notes but dreading the time when it would be my turn to share my vulnerable poem. I watched and listened as other brave souls poured their hearts out in front of everyone. I questioned why I couldn't do this. Then one day, I felt an urge stronger than my holding pattern of resistance. It was a powerful force stirred from the deep desire to do something different. Unsure of what came over me at that moment, I took the leap, raised my hand, and made my way to the front of the class to share. This was the first of my many breakthroughs. I figured I might as well make the most out of this experience. I was paying a ton of money for it after all.

Taking a long, deep breath, I mustered up courage. My hands were shaking and my voice was rattling, but somehow my heart was completely at peace. I read my poem to the class to best of my ability.

If I... I Will...
by Kristi Lee Schatz

If I dare to voice myself
I will shake.
If I dare to put my foot down
I will shake.
If I dare to speak up for what I know is right
I will shake and shake and shake.
But if my voice rattles
I'm OK.
And if my hands are shaking
It's alright.
I will not let myself break
I will NOT let myself break.
I will not let myself go unheard.
I will speak up and I will be shaking.
But I cannot, I WILL NOT let myself break.

Immediately after reading the poem I broke. And it was the best thing that could have happened to me. I let myself be vulnerable, seen, and heard. I cried and I was witnessed. I saw exactly how shut down I had become. This empowering moment fueled my desire to plunge deeper, to push against my edge of discomfort, to leap, leap, and leap some more. I was truly seen, validated, and unconditionally loved by complete strangers.

ART THERAPY - A FEAST FOR MY INNER CRITIC

Another semester rolled around and presented a feast for my inner critic. Art therapy was the topic in class. I always thought of myself as crafty, not artsy. I could hot glue the shit out of found objects, but drawing and painting with the intention of letting go of perfection, no friggin way!

"You want me to do what?
Draw my feelings…
What does that even mean?"

Yeah, it was that moment in my life. The moment when you take a deep breath, tune into your body, drop your entire awareness into sensation, and just pray that all the stuff you pushed down over the years doesn't come hurling out during class.

I sat on the floor in front a 20 x 20 sheet of paper, holding onto my least favorite color crayon, purple. Of course I let everyone else choose their color preference first. I was a people pleaser! Except I never seemed to please myself.

And there I was, eyes closed, purple crayon in hand, forced to connect with my body and draw my feelings. I was guided to simply observe the sensations in my body moment to moment and draw them on the paper. I was tempted to peak, knowing that what I was drawing was not going to meet the standards of my inner critic. I somehow thought that if I cheated I could fix the mistakes before anyone saw it. But the teacher was too close. I had to settle on whatever I had created.

We were then guided to observe our immediate reactions as we slowly opened our eyes and looked at our picture.

"Of course, you fucked it up," said the voice of my inner critic.

And in that moment I paused. "Why so mean?" I wondered. It's not that bad. But yet a part myself, as if on autopilot, was berating me, telling me I wasn't good enough, that people would judge me. I was the only one doing the judging.

My inner critic had gone too far. For Pete's sake, I was actually trying to better myself. How dare this voice tell me my efforts weren't good enough. I was ready to go to battle with this part of myself who was controlling my mind and belittling my worth. "Bring it on!"

I carried on, pushing edge after edge until I started to notice an unusual feeling in my body. It was one of self-acceptance. I began to notice that the old, invalidating voice in my head didn't snap back at me anymore. "Hmm... Where did it go?"

I was reprogramming myself. All those efforts to stop the deceptive automatic tapes were finally paying off. I was choosing to be a vulnerable badass and the logic of my inner critic was now unfounded. I was transforming before my own eyes.

PEAKS AND VALLEYS

Moving through the program was challenging. Every day I expanded into new, unseen parts of myself. I was beginning to realize the potential that I had always felt lingering deep within. My natural intuition, which had been fuzzy and sporadic, was becoming easier to access. I was finally breaking free from my old limiting self.

By the end of the first school year, I was becoming more comfortable with being uncomfortable. I was finding peace being authentically seen and expressing my deeper truths within the group. I had no idea how much I could change in just eight short months when I actually applied myself.

Moving into the second year I was on fire for the possibility of more change. My heart opened with the thought of going deeper, uncovering new layers of truth. I grew leaps and bounds because I now had the tools to move forward with more grace.

Unfortunately, my journey had a unique twist. During the height of this transformational process, my beloved life partner was not by my side. How could he be? I was gone 10-12 hours a day with two internships and living in fear that he wouldn't accept the new me when I got home. Shit, I didn't even know what that looked like yet. I was still in the cocoon. My cohort knew me better than my own husband. I spent much of the course processing this fact, but I was still ill equipped to effectively communicate this with him. My marriage was falling apart.

We had been forewarned that it was critical to include our significant others during this intense personal journey. The amount of transformation that was going to occur was certain to challenge the homeostasis of any relationship. I didn't listen.

Wherever you are on your path, I want to stress the importance of fully including your loved ones in on the journey. Relationships take authenticity and the ability to consciously respond to each other's peaks and valleys. Just because they aren't as interested or passionate in personal development doesn't mean they don't care. Finding compassion and unconditional love for who and where they are will free you from feeling like you have to change them. You don't. You are only responsible to yourself. I must have missed that class.

I was afraid to share the new parts of myself that were emerging for fear of being challenged and rejected. This was clearly related to my old emotional baggage about authenticity and not feeling good enough. I felt too fragile to face the possibility that my husband wouldn't like the new me. This lack of authentic communication festered in me like the plague, causing much unnecessary stress. I felt alone and didn't know what to do, so I just carried on, hiding my true self from the one I vowed to walk through life with. Unfortunately, I was still too unconscious to realize that I was simply repeating an old pattern.

The story ends in a heart-breaking divorce after graduate school. I wish I had been more self-aware at the time to understand how I was contributing to the relationship tension. I didn't know and it's OK. It was a hard lesson to learn and I used the experience as an opportunity to grow as a person. Talk about being a vulnerable badass - I just admitted that and I don't know you - I mean we're best playmates and all, but come on.

I share that story not to scare you, but to encourage you to stay in connection with your mate through this process. It could provide deeper intimacy and richness like you've never experienced before. That's my hope.

TAKING THE LEAP

If you're going to be a warrior for change it starts with you taking ownership of your life. It requires an understanding of what you really want to create and overcoming the blocks in your way. When you take a risk and face uncertainty, you will inevitable grow as a person. Whether you want to start a business, move to a different city, share your true feelings with others, or open your heart to a lover, you must be willing to accept vulnerability as a courageous path forward.

THE GLASSES OF LEIGH-ANN

The following interviewee is a mother who has had her own struggles with the five principles, especially vulnerability. She has agreed to share her challenges and story for the purpose of doing something different and stepping outside of her comfort zone - a true indicator of a vulnerable badass. Meet Leigh-Ann Sullivan.

Tell us a little about yourself.

I'm 36 years old and married to a handsome man with two incredible children. We are a military family so we move around quite a bit. If I could describe myself in three words I would say creative, adventurous and eccentric. I love music, photography and singing. If I were insanely rich, I'd pack up my family, homeschool my kids and travel around the world.

You recently told me that you are a master at hiding from yourself. Talk to us about that and your fears around vulnerability.

Until recently, I've spent my life trying to mold myself to fit perfectly into every situation. When that didn't work out, and it never does, I would run away. Instead of celebrating my authentic, vulnerable self, I had a mask for everything - perfect military spouse, perfect mom, perfect entertainer, perfect daughter. Now that I think about it, I wasn't even concerned with perfection. Instead, I was concerned that if anyone saw my brand of crazy, they wouldn't like me and I would be shunned from the pack. It is incredibly scary to realize that my vulnerable and trusting self is wide open for all the world to see and even more frightening that being open could destroy every wall I've built to protect myself.

When you read the first draft of this book, how did it impact you?

My first thought was, 'Holy fuck, everything is going to change now.' I had to sit quietly for a while and make the conscious decision to remove my masks. And what I saw underneath was so neglected and malnourished that I immediately wanted to build more fake masks that looked authentic and vulnerable, but not truly take the steps to transform. You, Kristi, have a way of calling me out on my bullshit. Five minutes with you talking about this book annihilated my walls and turned every mask into a puff of smoke.

Since reading it, how have you began to integrate the principles in your daily life?

After reading The Maju Mindset, I realized each day is all about perspective. Every experience or situation, from the mundane to the extraordinary, the exhilarating to the frightening, has something to teach me. I've learned to consciously approach difficult situations with love and openness, curiosity and sometimes humor. I just pop my Maju glasses on and explore.

You are a mother of two. What do you want your children to learn about authenticity and vulnerability?

I truly believe children are naturally authentic and vulnerable. We show them how to don masks and erect walls to hide behind because they learn by our example. As their mother, I can show them authenticity and vulnerability by embracing that in myself and my own actions. I can share their space, sit in trust with them and give them the encouragement to explore their feelings and fears without judgment or trying to immediately fix anything. It can be so easy for adults to brush off a child's feelings.

Is there anything else you'd like to share that might be valuable to someone afraid of taking a leap in their life?

Keep a journal. It sounds simple, but for me so many unexpected things came up after reading this book. I wish I had written those things down as they arose so I could explore them further. Now I write down quick notes for any sensations or situations I want to revisit to help aid in my own personal evolution. I've found that by writing it down, it's much easier for me to come from a perspective of love and curiosity, instead of a place of fear or avoidance. Eventually, you'll cease to immediately play the victim in your own life and that is an incredible space to find yourself.

FINE TUNING YOUR GLASSES

Yippee .. It's playtime! Today is going to be fun (well, as much fun as vulnerability can be). We're going to test your level of vulnerable badassery and I want you to bring all you've got to the playground - and remember, it's just me. I'm totally trustworthy and we're like best friends now, so let's go!

Play Date #3 – Admit It

Here's the deal: if you play, you win. If you don't, you lose. You can write your responses in this book, or in a journal where it stays hidden in a secret chamber until you're ready to embrace your badass self and share it with others. I'm cool with that. You can even set it on fire when you're done so no one EVER sees it. I'm just asking you to admit it. I don't care what you do with it afterward.

The most vulnerable thing I am willing to admit is: _____

_____

_____

_____

_____

_____

_____

_____

This makes me feel: _____

_____

_____

When I admit this my body responds in this way: _____

_____

_____

If I admit this to others, I'm afraid they will think: _____

_____

_____

If I could accept this, I would feel: _____

_____

_____

YOUR MISSION

The next time you feel a twinge of vulnerability, challenge yourself to stretch beyond your comfort zone and embrace your badassery. Look, you're not going to become a vulnerable badass by sitting on the couch and hiding. Get out there and show the world how awesome you are. Common side effects: Feeling more confident in who you are, tears followed by a sense of relief, temporary physical tension that will be released and make you feel lighter, happier, and pretty damn epic. Now get going, you vulnerable badass!

Lean In

By Kristi Lee Schatz

Lean in, I ask
For you will see
The freedom that comes
From allowing me to just be me.

My boundaries are clear, healthy, and defined,
So I ask you to lean in and see what you find.
Look not through the lens colored by time,
Or the perception and beliefs from your current paradigm.

I want to be seen, held, and heard in the present
For that is where I currently reside.
I invite you to swim in the possibility
That we are both part of the same tide.
Moving in and out, steady and ever flowing
We are collectively ebbing and hopefully growing.

I do not need your approval, admiration, or praise
Instead I seek connection with a present gaze.
Reflecting and owning that which is shown
Moment to moment, the sensation has grown.
I want to love and connect deeper than the sea
Allowing space for each of us to simply be.

Lean in, I ask
For I want to see
All of your beauty
Hidden away from me.

Maju Style

We don't fight life as it happens.

We flow through it with acceptance,

learning and growing along the way.

> Trust The Process

7

PRINCIPLE 4: TRUST

When I was at my deepest, darkest state, I had no trust in the process or myself. I believed I was all alone, disconnected from everyone and the universe. I was constantly getting in my own damn way because I felt like nothing ever quite worked out in my favor. I was a victim to circumstance and fought life at every turn. Everything changed when I learned how to surrender to what I could not control and allow the natural flow of what was to be. Sounds simple, right?

Trust is likely the hardest principle to grasp. We understand it on a conceptual level, but the application in daily life is something I imagine most people struggle with. We worry about how the future will unfold. We wish the past would have been different. We fear stepping outside of our comfort zone and trying something new. How much time and energy do you spend indulging a mindset of distrust?

Trust comes in many shades, shapes, and depths, mirroring the complexity of life's hurdles. Some days we have a sense of unwavering trust that everything is going to be OK. Other days we bitch and moan about why things didn't go our way. On some occasions we trust our intuition and other times we doubt it. This is life.

Everything is unfolding just at it is. You are simply responding to it. If you fight it, you will continue to struggle with it. If you accept it, you will move through it with more grace and ease.

No matter what circumstance you are presented with, it's an opportunity for you to be present to what is arising within you. Knowing this at a deep level means you shift your lens of focus from trying to fix what's happening out there, and instead ask yourself, what am I meant to learn from this experience?

Life is like school. If you're paying attention you will learn new information and skills. From time to time you will be tested on how well you really understand what you've been taught. Sometimes you ace your test and other times you don't. Every opportunity in your life is the same way. All circumstances are opportunities to practice what the universe has been trying to teach you. If you are continually finding yourself impatient, you are being tested on patience. The world isn't doing this to you, you're doing it to yourself. Until you can turn the mirror and look inwards you will always see the same thing. If your way is working for you, then great! But chances are you're not as happy as you desire and you're probably experiencing more tension than you'd like. If this is the case, then it might be time to pay attention and try something different.

If you give this principle attention, the energy will flow there. It may bring up fear, doubt, and concerns. That's OK. It's the process of shining light on the principles that matters. The layers will be revealed when you're paying attention in the moment.

When life comes along and tests you, see if you can move into a state of trust by bringing your full attention to the present moment. Then watch what happens. How does your mind respond? Does it negate the possibility immediately? Are you truly in the present moment or lost in your rambling thoughts? When you affirm with conviction that you trust this moment just as it is, can you feel your body respond? The more you redirect your attention to a trusting mindset, the easier it becomes to see the world through a different lens. It takes time and each moment is an opportunity to practice.

For me, meditation was the catalyst for developing trust. When I am present to my thoughts without attachment, they eventually dissipate. It's the pause between my thoughts where I sensed the deeper voice from my heart. For a while, I didn't want to listen because it meant I'd have to make some changes. But even when it was scary, I chose to listen. When I had the courage to pay attention, my body responded with a sense of knowingness and feeling that energized me. Overtime, I developed trust in this inner guidance speaking through me. My life would not be what it is today if my inner critic was still running the show. I trust that.

Sometimes it's necessary to take a leap of faith, and hope the net will be there to catch you, to catapult into a new reality. If your heart is strongly pulling you in a direction and you're clinging to your old emotional attachments, you're likely creating more suffering for yourself than you truly desire. Learning to trust your intuition by taking hundreds, or even thousands, of baby steps until you feel grounded is key to erasing the old mental pictures that stand in the way of the life you are deeply yearning for.

I have taken my fair share of leaps. Some were small, some were monumental. Some worked out exactly like I thought, others were more challenging. Each leap was an opportunity to practice trust and acceptance. No matter what the outcome, the process always helped me become a better person. The only way to cultivate deep seated trust is to surrender. Follow your heart, stay in the present moment, and know that fear is normal.

I recall many times having a strong feeling of fear overtake my body. Despite the uncomfortable feelings, I was aware that a deep part of myself was encouraging me to move forward. When I began to trust this inner voice, everything in my life began to change. Trust that I can open my heart and be in connection with that person. Trust that I can follow my passion and open that business. Trust that it's time for me to move on from this job and create something more fulfilling. Trust that sharing my deeper truth is OK, even if tension arises. Trust that I am exactly where I need to be.

It takes trust to be authentic and vulnerable. Trust that you won't beat yourself up if things don't go your way. Trust that you can handle uncertainty when it arises. Trust that your wings will appear after you leap off the cliff of uncertainty. It all boils down to perspective. If the mental pictures you play in your mind are shaded with doubt, you will not only see the world through that lens, but your level of trust will always be filtered through that perspective.

TRUSTING CONNECTION

Recently a dear friend and I had a moment of difference that could have caused us to easily disconnect from one another. I knew we had both flown over our edges while pointing fingers at each other on the way down. Yet I had a deep trust that addressing an uncomfortable topic would ultimately strengthen our connection and our individual development because we ultimately trusted the bond between us and we were willing to own our stuff.

In a text dialogue with her the following day, I told her, "This might sound crazy, but it's my truth. I will always love you unconditionally. We will challenge each other from time to time. We will dance in joy and wonderment often. We will mess up and have to process shit. We are on this roller coaster called life and we are both actively stretching ourselves and sometimes that means tension. We are strong enough to move through and grow from anything that arises between us, within us, or around us. It's all the same thing. I really trust the process of growth, however it unfolds. I want to see you in all your ways, vulnerable, closed, happy, angry, present, open, loud, quiet, silly, absent, and so on. I ask for you to also hold space for me to be those things, too. I'm far from perfect. I'm human as all hell. It's the process of the journey that is magical. The ups and downs that take us through the trenches together is where everything reveals itself. These are the moments we shine light on each other to grow. This is the space we hit our shit together. This is the process and we are lucky to have each other to go through it with consciously because most people don't have that. We get to be each other's walls from time to time and I think that is magical. I imagine that sounds crazy, but for me that is true. It's my perspective. I love you."

The response was a genuine, "I love you too. I trust you. I'm scared." We have moved past it with grace. We trusted our connection despite the tension and our initial habitual reaction to withdraw. We spoke our authentic truths from a place of personal ownership as much as possible and witnessed each other be vulnerable. A few hours later, we went to a skating rink for her daughter's birthday, hugged it out and danced our butts off as we tried to remember how to be a kid on wheels. This is life. We didn't push it down. We didn't placate each other. Sure, we both could have been more present to what was arising as the tension began to boil. Despite that, we trusted that speaking our vulnerable truths would pave the path for deeper connection. And it did.

THE GLASSES OF JORDAN

If there is one person who has coached me, modeled to me, and inspired me to be vulnerable, authentic, and trusting, it's this man. Meet Jordan Myska Allen. An author, facilitator, coach, and total vulnerable badass. He is truly changing the world simply by being himself. This is his perspective on trust.

Tell us a little about yourself

This is probably the hardest of all the questions to answers, because I am both very clearly defined and yet constantly changing. I love people, particularly watching them grow and discover something new, learn to love themselves, and engage the world with a sense of wonder and awe.

I also love truth, coffee, rock-climbing, and stories. Loving people and truth led me to Circling (a meditation on connection) and building a thriving online practice community around it.

Loving coffee and stories led me to four years of staying up late writing a zombie-apocalypse-road-trip meets integral-psychology novel.

What does trusting the process mean to you?

We get a simple choice to whatever comes up in our lives - resist it or accept it. I like to call this acceptance surrender, which is another way of saying trust the process. Surrender doesn't mean giving up, it means being honest about what's happening and your reaction to what's happening. It means being a yes to truth - a truth which might include your no. It means admitting that the vast majority of the process is utterly out of our control.

Think of a rainstorm: resisting the truth is like pretending it doesn't exist because you don't like being wet. Yet of course if you pretend it doesn't exist and stay outside, you'll end up soaking wet, exactly what you didn't want. If, on the other hand, you trust the process and accept the truth of the rainstorm (and the truth of your preference for being dry), you'll react in any number of simple ways to stay dry. How do you meet the rainstorms of your life's circumstances? How do you meet the rainstorms that arise in you?

What relationship do you see between fear, trust, and being present?

I see being present and trust as synonyms that both point toward living in full acceptance.

Fear is something you can be present to. Fear is something you can learn to trust. Fear is like an old friend who knows you well, and shows up at your doorstep with a gift. Think of a fear now - what is its gift for you? Can you invite this friend in, unwrapping the gift to see what it offers?. Now can you give it thanks, cherish the present and then ask it to leave?

What role does trust play in your life?

More and more I'm learning to listen and trust what arises in me. The words often surprise the hell out of me, but when I'm willing to share them they always bring me deeper into intimacy with life and reveal some new mystery.

What would you say to someone who is seeking to deepen their level of trust, but is having a challenging time?

I would encourage them to develop a relationship of genuine curiosity with their desire and their challenge. What is the challenge? What does it feel like? What gift is it offering? Where does it seem to be at odds with other parts of yourself? What about your desire to deepen into trust? Do you have a sense of your motivation? What resistance comes up when you imagine that trust?

FINE TUNING YOUR GLASSES

I think we only have two play dates left, which makes me feel sad. Luckily, I trust the time we had together was exactly what it needed to be, for better or for worse. I trust that the seeds planted have either enlivened your soul or pissed you off. I'm cool with either one, because I trust the process. I am speaking my truth and how you respond is up to you. I support you unconditionally and my team of badass facilitators and coaches are here to catch you if you want to dive deeper. We're all in this together. OK, enough grown up shit, back to playtime.

Play Date #4 – Free Time (sort of)

I'm going to switch things up here because I trust you are capable of defining your own rules (I'm so nice!) I've laid out a few prompts for you to simply write what ever comes to mind. You can go as deep or shallow as you'd like, it's your choice. My request is that you simply notice what arises moment to moment, but again, it's your rules this time. Happy writing, buddy!

I trust _____

_____

_____

_____

_____

I fear _____

_____

_____

_____

_____

I am resisting _____

_____

_____

_____

_____

I know _____

_____

_____

_____

_____

YOUR MISSION

Take time each day to see if you can truly surrender and let go of what you cannot control Because I'm willing to bet the only thing you actually have control of is your response. Everything else just is.

The Children Await
By Kristi Lee Schatz

The fire, it burns deep in my bones
Destroying the old and tarnishing the stones.
The weight I've carried for far too long
Is starting to shed revealing the strong.

The courage to surrender, leap and fly
Summons my warrior who has never died.
The vision of freedom and possibility to rise
Has awaken my soul to come alive.

I sense a truth hidden from my eyes
Awaiting my attention to reveal the wise.
It speaks with conviction, love and grace
Knowing I'm listening from an attentive place.

"You must nurture your Spirit and model to the children
For they are the ones who will influence the billions.
Get out of your way and learn something new
It's time to shift your limiting worldview."

Maju Style

If you're not going to lead with heart,
please don't lead at all.

> Be The Change

8

PRINCIPLE 5: ROLE MODELING

Authentic role modeling is about a self well-expressed. The way you show up, the grace in which you handle tough situations, and the permission you give yourself to be authentic and vulnerable can greatly influence another person.

It's not about giving unsolicited advice or thinking you know what is best for someone else. When your inner light shines on someone it helps them see themselves. You are not here to fix anyone. You are simply here to evolve and freely express yourself so that others may see the possibilities and the beauty of imperfection.

Role modeling in the maju way is about holding unconditional space for another person's experience. The deeper your inner dive, the easier it becomes to sit with another person without the need to change them. Your smile, eye contact, genuine curiosity, humility, and ability to truly listen can be a catalyst for others to feel seen and heard. As mentioned earlier, many of us have never felt truly seen, partly because we hide ourselves and partly because of the projections we experience from others.

The fifth principle of the Maju Mindset is about breaking this cycle. As you develop yourself and choose each moment to fully express, you will create a ripple effect around you.

We must not underestimate how much children look up to us as role models. It's not about what you say to them, but how your presence feels to them. Your inner world doesn't just create your reality, it shapes theirs as well. In order for us to create more "play space" for the next generation, we must nurture the personal development of the adults who can then consciously role model the infinite possibilities for our children.

Let's not forget that we are all tied together. Our shared human experience and the collective agreements we uphold for the system to function as it does are the threads that bind us.

What do you want the world to be like? Loving, accepting, kind? What about unlimited, authentic, vibrant, passionate, and forgiving? If you aspire to this, it's up to you to embody these for yourself first.

We've all felt restricted in some way or another. Many of us have adopted a psychology around lack, limitation, and scarcity that we unknowingly pass on to our children. This isn't intentional of course, but it is an unfortunate byproduct when we can't see our own habits and limitations. Communication patterns work the same way.

What I am about to say is by no means an attempt to blame you or say you are doing something wrong. We're all screwing this up together because no one taught us these things in the first place. Not because they didn't care, but because they didn't know. The question I invite you to sit with is, "How is my presence impacting the children of this world, and what am I willing to do about it from this moment forward?"

Children watch and learn constantly. They pick up on subtle cues from other people's interactions and develop a rulebook for what they view as acceptable and unacceptable behavior. They can feel when there is tension in a room and they watch how it's handled. They sense when someone close to them is lying and learn it's OK to lie. They observe their older brothers being told to toughen up and learn it's not OK for them to feel their feelings. Children of divorced parents may hear each other say mean things, trying to get the kids to take sides. How do you think this impacts our children? From teachers, to babysitters, police officers, parents, aunts, uncles, and celebrities, we're all contributing to the collective social consciousness and something isn't working.

Here are a some more examples of how we unknowingly pass on our way of being to our children:

- We tell our children to not take mean comments personally from the kids at school, yet we constantly bitch about what he said or she said that hurt our feelings.
- We tell our kids to be nice to each other, but they witness us talking behind people's backs.

- We tell our children or students to calm down and punish them for being reactive, yet we go into a complete state of reaction when we're upset with them, our spouse, or anyone else who triggers us.

- We ask them to be polite to adults, yet they see us being disrespectful all the time.

- We want our kids to feel safe to share their feelings with us, but we continually hold in our own emotions, which they can feel energetically.

- We scold them for outwardly aggressive behavior, but demonstrate that passive aggressiveness is fine.

- They learn how to be by the way we are being. Remember, your presence is your power. If you dislike the state you currently find the world in, then ask yourself how you can show up differently.

LET THE CHILDREN LEAD

Several years ago I was a counseling intern at an elementary school in a low income neighborhood plagued by gang violence, drugs, familial incarceration, and domestic abuse. Early on, I realized that my role wasn't to be another person in their life telling them they are doing it wrong. They were products of their environment and there was no way I could effectively reach into their family system and fix anything. That wasn't my job. My role was simply to love them unconditionally and model patience, acceptance, healthy boundaries, surrender, authenticity, and vulnerability. I had to trust that my presence alone could be enough to seed a possibility in their young minds.

It seemed like everyone in their lives, from friends, older siblings, extended family, and teachers were telling them how they should be and what was wrong with them. I took a different approach. I became a kid with them. I let them teach me. I watched as their imagination was granted full permission to explore. I asked questions out of genuine curiosity without any agenda. I selectively disclosed parts of my story that were relatable to show I understood and that I struggled too. I allowed them to be the expert on life, and you know what? I learned a lot. I learned they pick up on a gentle loving presence and soften their armor even if nothing is said. I learned that engaging them in their inner world not only helps them feel seen, but shows them how creative they really are. I learned that I had buried my inner child away from the world because I had to give this whole "adulting" thing a try. Look how well that turned out.

Beyond the heartache I experienced over and over again from listening to their stories, there was a valuable lesson about fully showing up.

You don't have to go out to the world with an agenda and create something profound. Simply allowing yourself to lead life with an open heart is enough to have an impact on the world around you. A genuine smile can brighten another person's day. Saying hello to a stranger can show them everyone isn't closed off. Asking for a hug instead of a hand shake can move you into a more intimate connection with the other person. Being of service to those in need can model care and support. Deeply listening to someone without the need to say anything can provide space for them to explore their inner world on their own. Making eye contact can show you are really present. Everyone will choose to show up differently in the world adding to the dynamic unfolding of consciousness on this planet. The question to ask yourself is, "What impact is my presence having on this world?"

Your authentic and loving presence alone is enough to create systemic change.

As you take responsibility for your well-being, choose to show up authentically, give yourself permission to be vulnerable, and learn to trust the process, you will reconfigure the lens through which you view the world and you will embody that which others yearn for.

This yearning is often subtle, stemming from deep within. Many of us are unaware of what we are missing until we see others standing authentically in their light and power. "If only I could be like that," we say quietly to ourselves, yet caving in to the programmed beliefs that keep us feeling small.

Role modeling isn't about putting yourself or anyone else on a pedestal. It's about simply showing up in life, owning your feelings and projections, and authentically connecting with those you encounter.

No matter where you are on your journey it's important to keep a beginners mind because you can always learn from another person's perspective. Opening yourself up to mentorship from others can provide additional support on your journey toward self-actualization. Learning from others who have walked in similar trenches can provide valuable insight about navigating life with as much grace as possible.

Collectively, we are a catalyst for societal change because we choose to reach out as a source of light to those we encounter. We recognize the self-inquiry journey never ends and the more we learn the more we can model. We know this isn't about perfection because showing the vulnerable parts of ourselves can be just as powerful as sharing the integrated parts. It's about modeling that it is OK not to be perfect. It demonstrates self-acceptance and ownership over our habitual ways of being, knowing we will continue to learn and grow. We choose to seed limitless possibilities in the young minds and water them with encouragement. The light within us that is no longer trapped behind the walls of societal conditioning will inevitably shine upon the seeds we've planted to help the next generation truly flourish.

Choose to take action. Reach out to local organizations that work with at risk children. Offer help to young adults who aspire to be like you. Create opportunities for young, budding entrepreneurs to shadow you at work to learn both the hard and soft skills of business. Start a support group for adolescents to share their experiences so they know they are not alone. Invite your friends to participate in events that bring young people together. Stand tall as a model and be genuine in your guidance.

Make different choices, show up authentically, and be the light you wish to see in the world. The next generation is counting on us.

THE GLASSES OF CELESTE

Meet Celeste Blackman. She is my mentor and the model I look to for guidance when I am in need of support. She embodies grace, freedom of authentic expression, playful professionalism, healthy boundaries, and humility. These are the qualities I personally wish to see flourish in the world and strive to integrate into my daily life. Her presence alone can shift the energy and emotion of an entire room.

Tell us a little about yourself.

I'm an international consultant, coach and trainer dedicated to supporting people in being their best selves. I'm acutely aware of how relationships impact our biology, and in so doing our feelings, our behaviors and the results that we attain. Our relationships can add energy and joy or make us tired and miserable. I've learned that through my choices I have a lot of power to influence the quality of the relationships in my life and thus the quality of my health and happiness.

I believe that we are better together and I am committed to

sharing with all who are interested what I have learned about building high-trust relationships. I have come to understand that the most important aspect of a life well-lived is the quality of the relationships that we have in our life. I want this for all, in our homes, our schools, and our communities.

While I've always been interested in human potential, I deepened my commitment to this work after suffering the loss of my home to a flood nearly 15 years ago. In the aftermath of this experience I came face to face with the challenges that disaster can wreak on a person, a couple, and a family. This experience deepened my understanding of the fragility of the human experience and how deeply we need one another. It increased my understanding that my experience and my own joy is a reflection of my inner world, irrespective of the circumstances that I find myself in. When my inner world is chaotic and fearful my outer world takes on those characteristics as well. When it is at peace and happy, I get to experience more joy and positive emotions. My capacity to shift my inner and outer state in a positive way begins with me and is aided exponentially when I engage with others with whom I feel happy, positive and energized. If I don't like the results I'm experiencing in my life, I benefit most from looking at the choices that I am making and who I'm hanging out with.

What does being an authentic role model mean to you?
It means actively and consciously showing up, paying attention and

being intentional about having a positive impact on others. It means recognizing that we have an impact on one another and being self-accountable for the quality of that impact.

What do you think is the most important aspect of being a mentor for others?

Being real. Being kind. Caring deeply.

What is emotional contagion and how does it impact those we encounter?

We are social animals with a social brain and we are wired to pick up on the feelings and emotions of others with whom we come in contact. Emotions can spread like a virus infecting others and contributing to the creation of either a positive or negative attitude and environment. The implications are huge. Our attitudes toward one another impact our willingness to cooperate, communicate, and work well together. Over time our mood and our attitude impacts our relationships, our health and well-being.

How do you think we can inspire the next generation to lead happy, healthy, and purpose-driven lives?

By seeking to lead happy, healthy and purpose-driven lives ourselves, we pave the way for those who follow to more easily build on our discoveries with their own, thus paving the way for the next generation to do the same. This evolutionary process can continue to adapt and improve on the previous generations' contributions, building an aspiring and conscious approach toward life and one another. We expedite the process by deliberately teaching useful skills and modeling effective behaviors.

What advice would you give to the next generation about successfully navigating life?

Engage in your life. Invest in your inner world as well as your outer world. You have been gifted with many forms of intelligence, seek to develop them all. Say yes to that which brings you joy and energizes you and no that which drains your energy and darkens your mood.

You are the co-founder of Green Zone Culture Group. What is the Green Zone and how can it help individuals personally and professionally?

The Green Zone refers to the interpersonal space created between two or more people. The purpose of the Green Zone Culture Group is to cultivate Green Zone Thinking; a cooperative mindset that recognizes that we are better together. It is this quality of thinking that enables people to work better together, build trust and connection and find increased energy, joy and aliveness at work and in life.

People operating with Green Zone Thinking recognize that emotions are contagious and that we are each responsible for the emotions we carry and spread. They recognize that emotions are powerful precursors to action and it is through our actions that we create results. People using Green Zone Thinking actively, consciously and responsibly seek to create environments that invite others to feel positive and supported. Green Zone Thinking is the foundation for building Green Zone Cultures, positive interpersonal environments characterized by safety, trust and caring. These environments support people in optimizing their personal and professional capabilities.

FINE TUNING YOUR GLASSES

It's our last play date together... Let's be awesome!

Play Date #5 – Be Awesome. Be Limitless.

My rules: dream big and don't limit yourself. Anything is possible. The objective is to step out of your own damn way and imagine what might be possible for your life. What would the world look like if you fully showed up? How could your presence shift your community? If you could be a badass role model, what would that look like? It's time to be limitless and I want you to bring it. Go!

When I'm fully shining my brightest I: _____

_____

My passion is: _____

_____

My purpose is: _____

_____

The thing I love most about myself is: _____

_____

When I dream into what my life could look life I envision: _____

_____

_____

_____

I am truly limitless and I know I will create: _____

_____

_____

When I think about how my presence impacts the world around me,

I want to show up this way: _____

_____

_____

When I'm feeling low or vulnerable, I commit to: _____

_____

_____

I want future generations to know: _____

_____

_____

The next steps for my life are: _____

_____

_____

_____

I am a badass because: _____

_____

_____

You rock buddy! Best friends for life!

9

THE MAJU MINDSET IN EVERYDAY LIFE

These perspectives were only a faint idea of possibility for me just a short while ago. Now, they are my truths. They are integrated into the fabric of my being and are what inspire me to wake up each and every morning with a sense purpose. It doesn't mean I don't feel overwhelmed by fear, sadness, or doubt from time to time. It happens. It's part of the process. But I'd say 90 percent of my life is filled with more highs than lows because I've made the choice to evolve on purpose and remain present in the moment to whatever is arising within me. I overcame severe depression and debilitating anxiety because I took action daily to rework my inner world.

Life is a roller coaster and the more tools you have to gracefully handle issues when they arise, the quicker you'll be back up and running for another thrilling ride. Simply love yourself through it and draw upon the perspectives you've gathered to apply when needed. You may feel pain, sadness, and anger every so often, but it doesn't mean anything is wrong with you. Simply acknowledge it, find your sense of acceptance and curiosity about the opportunity at hand, and get to know that part of you.

A common issue I've noticed in the personal growth world is the notion of bypassing. We assume we always have to think positively and when a part of ourselves is frustrated or not happy we do whatever we can to push it away and just focus on the positive. But what happens to the part of you that had that less than desired perspective and reaction? It apparently didn't dissolve because it keeps popping up. When you notice a similar reaction occurring time and again, I recommend placing your attention on the part of yourself that feels that way rather than bypass it. It does no good to judge yourself for the feelings you are having. Shining a light with curiosity and non-attachment to a particular outcome can help you better understand the many parts of you. Being present to your feelings fosters greater self-awareness and allows you to consciously see other perspectives.

GETTIN' YOUR MAJU ON

Let's look at a few scenarios where the Maju Mindset can be applied to your everyday life.

You're stuck in traffic – A part of you feels frustrated, like the world is out to get you because once again, nothing ever seems to go your way. You're going to be late and this isn't how you wanted to spend your time. Sure, that's one part of you and it's important to recognize it. But what other perspectives lie at your disposable in this moment when you take your blinders off? One option is to view this as a great opportunity to apply trust in the process. For some reason this happened and it's actually not the end of the world. See if you can become aware of the part of you that wants to make this a bigger deal than it is and choose amusement. You can use this moment as an opportunity to practice mindfulness, which can impact the rest of your day.

Fussy children in the back seat – Sure, part of you may want to pull over the car, wave your hands in the air, and possibly even put duct tape over their mouths to help ease your inner tension (don't do that). Rather than go into complete reaction, see if you can return to your center through deep breaths. See if you can address the situation through a calm presence. I'm not saying children shouldn't be disciplined, but just notice if your reason for disciplining them has more to do with what's arising within you. It's difficult to be present to a child's actual needs when your inner world is in a state of chaos too.

Your boss is being an ass – You go into work ready to take action and alas, your boss is being a jerk. A part of you may want to tell him off, throw all his neatly filed papers on the floor, and run to everyone and bitch about what an ass he's being. Or perhaps you want to run away and hide in your cubicle, silently beating him up with your thoughts. Let that feeling within yourself be OK. Notice what's coming up for you and see if you can bring yourself fully to the present moment to reduce your overactive nervous system response. No one likes to be bullied, or treated poorly. Let's try this perspective on for size: You can't control their emotions. Maybe their home life sucks. Maybe they are under extreme pressure from their boss. Maybe they don't have the tools to effectively handle the stress they feel in their own lives. Maybe you're projecting onto them because you didn't like their response. See if you can move into a space of curiosity and compassion for them. This is not to say you should stay in a work environment that is toxic and unhealthy, but first see if you can use this experience as an opportunity to practice your new tools. Perhaps you may gain a deeper insight and sense of clarity about the best option to make for yourself once you're more fully present and not in a state of reaction. It's a possibility. You may decide it's time to calmly sit down with your boss and share your authentic feelings from a space of personal ownership rather than blame. Maybe you'll discover a part of yourself that has had unhealthy boundaries and now is the time to make an adjustment to how you want to be in relationship with others. Every scenario and work culture is different and there is not a one size fits all answer here; but if you choose to turn the mirror toward yourself first, you'll be better positioned to address the issue from a place of self-awareness.

Your mother-in-law is coming to town – She's a nice lady and means well, but boy does she know how to get under your skin and push your buttons. You spend a week dreading her arrival, playing out every worse case scenario in your mind. As her plane pulls into the gate, you put on your most loving mask and try to pretend the movies in your mind aren't playing on a loop. The first night goes well, but the next morning she's rearranging your stuff, telling your children what to do, and playing overprotective mom to your spouse. For Pete's sake, this is your role, right? How do you handle this? Well, you could choose to do what you've always done. Or maybe you could try this perspective on for size: My mother-in-law is coming and we haven't always gotten along, but I wish we could. Rather than dreading her arrival, perhaps I'll focus on myself with curiosity and acceptance and stay present to the part of me that is frustrated. Maybe I'll even set a play date with myself to have a dialogue with the part that is dreading the next seven days. Perhaps the buttons she so easily bumps up against are within myself. Maybe I should consciously lean into it before she comes to understand the mechanism so I'm not over sensitive. Can I choose to embody unconditional love for the part of myself that isn't at peace? When she I arrives, I don't have to feel compelled to put on an act because I'm present and genuinely in a state of love for myself and my family. My mother-in-law is who she and is doing the best with the tools she has and perspectives she chooses. She's different from me and that is OK. I understand she's excited to see her child and grandchildren.

She's been waiting all year to play the role of mother and grandmother. Maybe this time I'll let her and see if I can find my amusement when my shit comes up. Perhaps this time, instead of going into reaction when I notice she crosses my boundaries, I'll sit down with her and share my authentic truth. I want to be closer with her and I'm ready to break the cycle that we seem to be caught up in. I know it starts with me taking the first step and I'm committed to doing something different this time. It's a possibility.

NEXT STEPS

Here is my invitation to you: step forward. Developing yourself is the greatest gift you can give to the world. The only person you are competing against is yourself. Every day is an opportunity to step out of your old way of thinking and try something new. What do you want to create for your life? Why do you want this? How do you want to feel? What fears, doubts, and beliefs stand in your way of achieving this? Choose in this moment to take one step forward in your mindset and say, "I can have this." Setting goals is more than just describing what you want. You must feel it, own it, and believe it's a possibility. Your mindset must be coated with the knowingness that even when fear and doubt arises, you can still step forward. Taking personal responsibility for what you are creating from this moment forward is the maju way. Will you listen and honor your deeper truths? Will you show the world your unique self? Will you step out of your comfort zone and grow? Will trust the ebbs and flows of life? Will you be a source of light in the world? This is your life. Create it in the way that feels right for you. Your mindset is the doorway to your greatness. The children are waiting for us to take that step. What will you choose?

BE AWESOME

I am going to leave you with this: happiness is not for wimps.

Let's face it, happy people are awesome. Not the superficial happiness that comes from showering yourself with new stuff, pretending to be perfect in order to receive praise, or making a ton of money at a soul-sucking job. Rather, it's the deep-seated happiness that develops through courageous self-observation leading to inner strength and trust in whatever unfolds.

To know oneself in a society that does not value authentic and vulnerable expression poses many challenges for our genuine sense of happiness. Instead of taking time for self-reflection, we seek happiness from outside ourselves only to be disappointed by what the world cannot provide. The path of embracing our imperfections, accepting ourselves as we are, and striving to become a better person each day is not for wimps.

One must not dismiss the courage it takes to closely examine your life, knowing that the odds of having to face your inner demons are high. But until you turn your attention inward, you shall remain at the mercy of your unprocessed stuff, which unconsciously directs your daily mental, emotional, and behavioral responses.

The old paradigm of mocking personal growth work is quickly fading from sight as more people are experiencing profound shifts toward true happiness. When we awake from the illusion that we are powerless and realize that every moment offers an opportunity to observe ourselves and adjust our responses, we begin to understand just how disconnected we have been. This awakening opens the door for us to experience profound self-love, joy, and inner peace, as well as empowers us with the ability to surrender to what we can't control.

So, ask yourself, "How happy am I, truly?" Are you content with life, overwhelmed with joy or stress, following your bliss, or wishing circumstances would change in your favor? Is your level of happiness unwavering or easily affected by the actions of others?

If your answer is less than ideal, please do not fret, my new found friend. The noble path toward rediscovering yourself may be frightening at first, but it will also be invigorating, enlightening, and can move you closer to your true self and lasting happiness. Whether you join a local meditation class, attend an inspiring conference, or sample the top personal development books on the market, the goal is simply to slow down, quiet your mind, and listen for your inner aha's that will empower you on the road ahead. Be bold, be strong, and just be you.

With Love, Kristi Lee Schatz

Thank you to everyone who offered contributions to The Maju Mindset. If you are interested in learning more about the science supporting the mind-body connection, please be sure to check out the book written by Keith Holden, MD, *Power of the Mind in Health and Healing.*

---

[1] Bhasin MK, Dusek JA, Chang BH, et al. *Relaxation response induces temporal transcriptome changes in energy metabolism, insulin secretion and inflammatory pathways.* PLoS ONE. 2013;8(5):e62817.

[2] Kaliman P, Alvarez-lópez MJ, Cosín-tomás M, Rosenkranz MA, Lutz A, Davidson RJ. *Rapid changes in histone deacetylases and inflammatory gene expression in expert meditators.* Psychoneuroendocrinology. 2014;40:96–107.

[3] Dusek JA, Otu HH, Wohlhueter AL, et al. *Genomic counter-stress changes induced by the relaxation response.* PLoS ONE. 2008;3(7):e2576.

[4] Bhasin MK, Dusek JA, Chang BH, et al. *Relaxation response induces temporal transcriptome changes in energy metabolism, insulin secretion and inflammatory pathways.* PLoS ONE. 2013;8(5):e62817.

[5] Creswell JD, Irwin MR, Burklund LJ, et al. *Mindfulness-Based Stress Reduction training reduces loneliness and proinflammatory gene expression in older adults: a small randomized controlled trial.* Brain Behav Immun. 2012;26(7):1095–101.

[6] Black DS, Cole SW, Irwin MR, et al. *Yogic meditation reverses NF-κB and IRF-related transcriptome dynamics in leukocytes of family dementia caregivers in a randomized controlled trial.* Psychoneuroendocrinology. 2013;38(3):348–55.

[7] Lazar SW, Kerr CE, Wasserman RH, et al. *Meditation experience is associated with increased cortical thickness.* Neuroreport. 2005;16(17):1893–7.

[8] Luders E, Cherbuin N, Kurth F. *Forever Young(er): potential age-defying effects of long-term meditation on gray matter atrophy.* Front Psychol. 2014;5:1551.

[9] Wood, A.M., Maltby, J., Linley, P.A., Joseph, S. (2008). *The Authentic Personality: A Theoretical and Empirical Conceptualization and the Development of the Authenticity Scale.* Journal of Counseling Psychology, Vol. 55, No. 3, 386.

[10] Horney, K. (1951). *Neurosis and human growth.* London: Routledge.

[11] May, R. (1981). *Freedom and destiny.* New York: Basic Books.

[12] Rogers, C. R. (1961). *On becoming a person: A therapist's view of psychotherapy.* London: Constable.

[13] Winnicott, D. W. (1965). *The maturational processes and the facilitating environment.* New York: International Universities Press.

[14] Yalom, I. D. (1980). *Existential psychotherapy.* New York: Basic Books.

[15] Schmid, P. F. (2005). *Authenticity and alienation: Towards an understanding of the person beyond the categories of order and disorder.* In S. Joseph & R. Worsley (Eds.), *Person-centred psychopathology* (pp. 75– 90). Ross-on-Wye, England: PCCS Books.

[16] Baumeister RF, Leary MR. (1995). *The need to belong: desire for interpersonal attachments as a fundamental human motivation.* Psychol Bull. May, 1995;117(3):497-529.

[17] Mengers, Abigail A., (2014). *The Benefits of Being Yourself: An Examination of Authenticity, Uniqueness, and Well-Being"*Master of Applied Positive Psychology (MAPP) Capstone Projects. Paper 63. http://repository.upenn.edu/mapp_capstone/63

[18] Dern, N (2010, March 5). *Sub-Personalities: Who's Calling The Shots?* Huffington Post. Retrieved from http://www.huffingtonpost.com/natasha-dern/sub-personalities-whos-ca_b_447845.html

[19] Boileau, B. *Sub-personalities and authenticity: A Model of Intervention in Spiritual Direction.* (pp. 30). Retrieved from http://www.theway.org.uk/Back/481Boileau.pdf.

Made in the USA
Middletown, DE
17 October 2016